TAKE YOUR CHURCH'S PULSE

10 VITAL SIGNS OF A HEALTHY CHURCH

TIM KOSTER & JOHN WAGENVELD

Healthy Conversations
For Your Church

Dedication

To *Corrie Lenting.*

And to the church planters, partners, staff, volunteers and friends who make up the Multiplication Network.

We are in this together!

Published by:
MULTIPLICATION NETWORK MINISTRIES (MNM)
22515 Torrence Ave., Sauk Village, IL 60411, USA
www.multiplicationnetwork.org
708-414-1050

TAKE YOUR CHURCH'S PULSE

@ 2014 Tim Koster and John Wagenveld

PRINTED IN UNITED STATES OF AMERICA

Design by Rommel Salazar & Joshua Duque

CONTENT

PREFACE

The church exists by mission as fire exists by burning.
- "Emil Brunner"[1] -

This book presents ten vital signs of a healthy church: five key commitments and five key functions. It then introduces you to a church health diagnostic tool you can apply to your setting. Thousands of pastors and leaders around the world have found this framework helpful in organizing the ministry and mission of the local church. This book and the free diagnostic tool it presents are most useful if accompanied by a robust engagement in conversations. We trust that humble, prayerful, and courageous men and women discussing these ten vital signs will be led by the Holy Spirit to discern a preferred future for your community of faith.

A healthy community of faith is rooted first of all in the character and nature of God. It understands its mission and purpose in the world and organizes its life and work to be faithful and effective in its context. No one of these vital signs stands alone. It is the combination of factors that together make up a faithful and fruitful organism, the living Church of our Lord Jesus Christ. There is no magic in the number ten, but for teaching purposes it has worked quite well in different cultural contexts in providing ideas and a language for discussing important issues in congregational life and mission.

The intended audience for this book is any pastor, leader, or church member who is interested in having healthy conversations with others to strengthen his or her community of faith. On occasion we address church planters as well since this booklet will be used to plant churches in developing nations around the world. We intentionally try to keep the wording simple and accessible and draw ideas from the schools of church growth, church health, and missional church. We wish for the reader to know that we are most interested in the conversation that, prayerfully led by the Holy Spirit, ensues among church leaders and entire congregations that use it. For that reason we put a part of the survey, Take Your Church's Pulse (TYCP), and a conversation starter at the end of each chapter.

Here are some suggested ways in which you can use this book:

- Read it simply as food for thought.
- Use it in small group study or discussion.
- Read it to consider the TYCP survey for your congregation.
- Use it to start a strategic planning process using the TYCP tools.

It is our prayer that your faith community might find joy and purpose in working through this tool by having vigorous conversations that lead to meaningful change and healthy congregations.

Tim Koster & John Wagenveld

> God's intent was that now, **through the church**, the manifold wisdom of God should be made known to the rulers and authorities in the heavenly realms, according to his eternal purpose which he accomplished in Christ Jesus our Lord.
>
> **Ephesians 3:10-11**

"Through the church…" What a key phrase. Through the church God is unveiling his redemptive purposes in the world. Through the church he is revealing his manifold wisdom. Through the church he is declaring the good news of salvation in Christ Jesus. Through the church God is demonstrating the reality of his transforming power. Through the church God lays claim to the kingdom that was inaugurated in the life and ministry of Jesus Christ. Through the church God models a vision for what life can be under the Lordship of Christ. Through the church God communicates redemption, brings restoration, and provides a foretaste of the community that works with hope as it anticipates a new heaven and a new earth. The main actor is God. The Church is his agent.

The full scope of the New Testament highlights the reality that God hasn't called and redeemed his people simply for their own benefit. He has chosen the church to change the world. Through the church, as believers gather in a community of faith, others get a glimpse of the way life is supposed to be. It is visible in the way husbands and wives treat each other, the way children are raised, and the way neighbors look out for each other. It is evident in how the elderly are respected and the disabled are nurtured. It is witnessed in vocations and work places where the shalom of God is demonstrated. It is displayed in the dignity extended to the poor and the struggling. It is manifested in the prophetic call to establish justice in society in ways that protect the most vulnerable.

God's intentions for the church are huge, particularly when we stop to recognize that the church is a gathering of very ordinary people, complete with warts and blemishes. To even begin to live out God's dreams for us, we require an infusion of the life-giving Spirit and an awareness of how he has gifted us and where we need more of his healing grace.

The graphic below helps us understand that the Church is a creation of the Spirit and has its essence in the nature and character of God. When God is recognized as being the primary agent in mission and that the gospel is for the sake of the world, only then does our human effort, led by the Spirit, make sense. Therefore, a conversation on healthy church first recognizes the active agency of God through the Spirit within all of creation and through the Church toward the world. After that comes the purpose, function, and organization of the communities of faith. These participate with God in his mission.

**THE REDEMPTIVE REIGN OF GOD
THROUGH THE CHURCH IN MISSION**

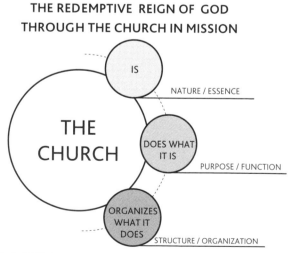

Adapted from Craig VAN GELDER, *The Essence of the Church: A Community Created by the Spirit*. Grand Rapids: Baker Book House, 2000.

Viewing the church as the Body of Christ gives us a helpful way to develop an awareness of how the Holy Spirit is at work in a congregation. When someone visits the doctor, the appointment always begins with the collection of certain basic data: pulse, temperature, blood pressure, oxygen levels, weight, blood sugar, and cholesterol levels, etc. Those simple tests offer insight as to what is happening inside the body. If something is wrong, the tests also offer direction as to treatment—or at least the next round of tests.

In the same way, there are 10 simple vital signs that offer insight into the health of a congregation. The list is neither definitive nor exhaustive, but it is sufficient to recognize a movement of the Spirit or a problem that needs to be addressed. Every church lives out these vital signs at some level. A healthy church will have them operating in an effective and balanced way. The context will determine the form in which they are expressed. The ten vital signs are:

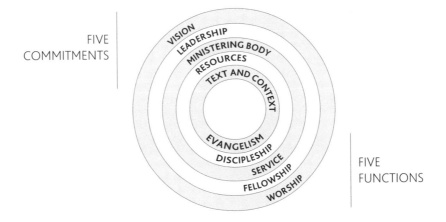

In the following pages, we discuss each vital sign and explain how it contributes to greater ministry effectiveness. These vital areas of a healthy church can be divided into two parts. In the first part, we present the five essential commitments, defined by the Spirit, that every congregation should have. The second part explains the five vital functions, led by the Spirit, that should be considered as areas in which the church must work. All of these arise from God's command to proclaim, announce, and embody the good news of the already present reality of God's kingdom in Jesus Christ, empowered by the Holy Spirit, which will bring transformation to all areas of life for God's glory.

[For formal definitions of CHURCH, see the appendix section.]

10 CHARACTERISTICS OF A HEALTHY CHURCH FROM THE NEW TESTAMENT

FIVE COMMITMENTS	FIVE FUNCTIONS
CLEAR AND INSPIRING VISION • Mtt. 9:36-38; Luke 4:14-21 • Acts 1:8 • 2 Cor. 5:14-21; 2 Tim. 2:15, 22-24; 2 Tim. 4:1-7	**COMPELLING WITNESS** • Matt. 28:18-20; Luke 24:45-48 • Acts 5:42; Acts 10:34-43 • Rom. 10:13-15; 2 Cor. 4:5; 2 Cor. 5:20-21
MOBILIZING LEADERSHIP • Mark 10:42-45; John 13:1-17 • Acts 6:1-7; Acts 13:1-3; Acts 20:28-31a • 2 Cor. 2:17; 2 Cor. 4:1-2; Eph. 4:11-13	**COMPREHENSIVE DISCIPLESHIP** • Matt. 28:18-20 • Acts 17:11; Acts 19:9b-10 • 2 Tim. 2:2; Titus 2:7-8; 2 Pet. 3:18
MOTIVATED MINISTERING BODY • Luke 10:1-2 • Acts 6:1-7 • Rom. 12:4, 6-8; Eph. 4:11-13; 1 Pet. 4:10-11	**COMPASSIONATE SERVICE** • Matt. 6:1-4; Matt. 20:25-28; Matt. 25:31-46 • Acts 6:1-7; Acts 20:35 • Gal. 6:10; Heb. 13:16; James 1:22, 27; James 2:14-17
PROPER STEWARDSHIP OF RESOURCES • Luke 19:11-26 • Acts 2:44-46; Acts 4:32-35 • 1 Cor. 4:2; 2 Cor. 8:1-7	**CARING AND WELCOMING COMMUNITY** • John 17:20-23 • Acts 2:42, 44 • 1 Cor. 12:25b-26; Gal. 6:1-2; Eph. 4:32; Heb. 10:24-25; 1 John 1:7
INTEGRATION OF TEXT AND CONTEXT • John 1:14 • Acts 17:18-28 • 1 Cor. 9:19-23	**DYNAMIC WORSHIP AND PRAYER** • Matt. 28:8-9; Luke 24:50-52; John 4:19-26 • Acts 13:2 • Heb. 12:28-29; Rev. 5:9-14

FIVE KEY COMMITMENTS
OF A HEALTHY CHURCH
PART I

The first five indispensable *commitments* upon which a healthy church is built are:

1. a clear and inspiring *vision,*
2. a mobilizing *leadership,*
3. a motivated *ministering body,*
4. the proper stewardship of *resources,* and
5. the integration of the *text* to the *context.*

These will be covered in this section. The remaining five vital signs of a healthy church will be dealt with in the next section as *functions* of a healthy church.

First Key Commitment
A CLEAR AND INSPIRING VISION

Vision allows the church to see clearly what God wants it to be and do, so that the Body of Christ may be unified as it gives witness to God's new creation in its community.

What is a vision?

A vision is a clear mental picture of a preferred future. It is not a pithy slogan or motto on a T-shirt or mug. It is not a generic paragraph fitting every other church in the community. It is not a strategic goal to accomplish in the next 1-2 years.

A motto can be a great marketing tool, particularly if it distills the essence of your vision in a memorable fashion. It can serve as a shorthand descriptor of your vision, but great vision will be too rich and deep to fit in that small of a bottle.

A vision for one congregation may overlap the visions of other churches in similar circumstances. After all, we serve one Savior and the same Scriptures shape our congregations. Yet God has a unique and special role for each body of believers.

A vision will ultimately work itself out into specific goals, but instead of bogging down in the details, it holds out a dream of what could be as we join God in bearing witness to the full reality of God's kingdom in our midst.

A vision is a congregation's answer to the question, "What is that preferred future God is leading us into? God has us here in this place, at this time, with these particular people, gifts, and challenges. What is that clear mental picture of the place where God is taking us as a congregation?"

Arriving at such an answer is challenging for two reasons: the church is as complex as the people in it and God doesn't clue us into everything he is up to. We see only in part. Still we are never clueless.

We begin at the intersection of three lines:

- the scriptural descriptions of the church and its purpose,
- the unique gifts and passions of church members, and
- the opportunities and challenges of the community.

3 KEY INGREDIENTS IN CLARIFYING YOUR VISION

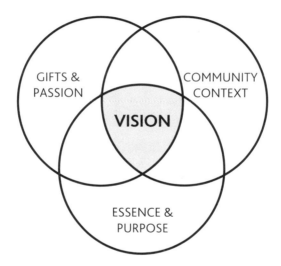

Or to put it slightly differently: What has God created the church to be and what is God's general purpose for the church as a whole? How has he uniquely equipped us as a local body? Where has he placed us in this broken world?

When we can state a clear answer to those questions, the resulting vision will propel us to pursue Christ and his kingdom. The element of vision has to do with perspective, with how we "see" our role within the greater purposes of God for our community.

Robert Fulgham tells the story of a traveler from Italy who came to see the construction of a great church in the French town of Chartres... Arriving at the end of the day, he went up to the site just as the workmen were leaving. He asked one man, covered with dust, what he did there. The man replied that he was a stonemason. He spent his days carving rocks. Another man, when asked, said he was a glassblower who spent his day making slabs of colored glass. Still another workman replied that he was a blacksmith who pounded iron for a living. Wandering into the deepening gloom of the unfinished edifice, the traveler came upon an older woman, armed with a broom, sweeping up the stone chips and iron shavings and glass shards from the day's work. "What are you doing?" he asked. The woman paused, leaned on her broom, and looking up at the high arches, replied, "Me? I'm building a cathedral for the Glory of Almighty God."[2] That's vision.

A clear and inspiring vision empowers the church by providing urgency and unity. The church without vision is not only blind. It is also prone to being shaped primarily by tradition and surrounding culture. It ends up drifting without direction, comfortable and complacent. It has no sense of urgency to carry out the task to which God has called it. It is like the frog in the illustration that George Barna describes in *The Frog in the Kettle*.[3] If we put a frog in a pot with boiling water, the frog will immediately jump out. However, if we put a frog in warm water and increase the heat little by little, the frog will stay there, comfortable and content until it dies, without realizing the danger. That is what happens with the church that is too comfortable and at home in its context—it doesn't realize that its lack of awareness is killing it little by little. This is the great advantage of new congregations—new churches generally begin with great enthusiasm and with a contagious vision. Church planters should take advantage of this moment to further develop that vision and to communicate it with conviction to prospective leaders and the broader community.

THE DIFFERENCE BETWEEN VISION AND MISSION

A VISION STATEMENT	A MISSION STATEMENT
DEFINITION	
A vivid description or image of how the world will be different if we are obedient to God's call. It works like the North Star to keep the church moving in the right direction to achieve its mission.	A brief paragraph that tells how your church or organization achieves its vision. It gives "legs and feet" to the vision. Your unique answer to the questions: • Why are we here as a congregation? • What are we here to be or to do?
KEYWORD	
THE RESULT	YOUR TASK
EXAMPLE	
We envision a community where Christ and his church are viewed with honor and respect because all of its citizens have been touched by the grace, the love, and the service of our members in the name of Jesus.	We exist to proclaim the gospel in word and deed; to grow in discipleship and fellowship; and to worship God.

Another danger of not having a clear vision is that in the absence of visionary leadership, people will fill the vacuum with their own visions. More than one focused vision causes division (divided vision). A clear vision puts every member of the congregation on the same page. It draws people together and aligns the congregation so that each member can serve in ways that build the Body of Christ (cf. Ephesians 4:1-16).

Beyond being clear, the vision must be true. It must fit the congregation. That is why it is so important to avoid the temptation to "borrow" a vision statement from another congregation, no matter "the success" of the other congregation. Using someone else's vision statement is like wearing someone else's clothes. It won't fit your body and it won't fit your personality. Your vision must capture a dream that God has already placed in your hearts in order to provide unity and urgency.

In *Shaping Things to Come*, Frost and Hirsch write:

> Considered philosophically, all that a great visionary leader does is awaken and harness the dreams and visions of the members of a given community and give them deeper coherence by means of a grand vision that ties together all the "little visions" of the members of the group. The fact remains that no one will be prepared to die for my sense of purpose in life. She or he will die only for her or his own sense of purpose. My task as a leader is to so articulate the vision that others are willing to embed their sense of purpose within the common vision of the community. Only if they think that the common vision legitimizes their vision will they be motivated by the leader's vision.[4]

Normally the vision is the first factor to consider when evaluating a ministry's progress. In the sport of soccer, midfielders are the strategic motor of the team. Midfielders link all the players together to both defend and attack. Often, the play in the midfield wins or loses games. The importance of the vision of a congregation is similar to the strategic importance of the midfield. Just as inadequate midfield execution causes problems for a soccer team, many of the problems that arise in new congregations arise from an inadequate vision. Winning teams and healthy congregations will have a clear and inspiring vision.

In our More Churches, Stronger Churches trainings, we teach eight key elements for a vision:

EIGHT KEY ELEMENTS OF VISION
• It projects a clear framework of an ideal future.
• It focuses on the future through God's eyes and provides direction.
• It is based on the redemptive purposes of God.
• It does not conform to the status quo.
• It requires faith. It is ambitious, yet realistic.
• It communicates clearly to others.
• It motivates people to act. It provides a sense of urgency.
• It is a shared vision.

Biblical Examples

In the Bible, we have clear examples of the vision God gives to those whom he calls. Adam and Eve had specific assignments to which God called them. The Cultural Mandate to fill the earth and subdue it as stewards of all created things was no small job. Even after the Fall, God continued to draw up plans for humankind. Everything starts with God's purposes for his people. In Genesis 12:1-3, God calls Abram and orders him:

> *"Leave your country, your people and your father's household and **go to the land I will show you**. I will make you into a great nation and I will bless you; I will make your name great, and you will be a blessing. I will bless those who bless you, and whoever curses you I will curse; and all peoples on earth will be blessed through you."*

Then in **Genesis 13:14-18** God says:

> *"Lift up your eyes from where you are and look north and south, east and west. All the land that you see I will give to you and your offspring forever. I will make your offspring like the dust of the earth, so that if anyone could count the dust, then your offspring could be counted. Go, walk through the length and breadth of the land, for I am giving it to you." So Abram moved his tents and went to live near the great trees of Mamre at Hebron, where he built an altar to the LORD.*

In these passages, God is the one who orders people to lift up their eyes to see what he will show them. God is the one who gives the vision of what to do. It is after God has shown us something that he tells us to get up—and then we can build. A good example of this process in the Old Testament is the story of Nehemiah. Nehemiah's heart was broken over the shattered city of Jerusalem. Even though work was proceeding in a limited fashion on individual buildings, the city itself was broken, bruised, and naked without its walls. The walls served as a symbol of strength and as a covering for the parts of the city that still needed restoration. After a season of prayer, Nehemiah shared his vision of a restored city with the king, then the city officials, and finally the people. With unity and urgency, they built the walls in the face of stiff opposition. It was a vision for their ability to live, serve, and worship God as God's covenant people.

Even more helpful are the epistles written to specific congregations. The visions in those letters were unique to the specific congregations who received them. Most wouldn't fit on a bumper sticker. Yet they are clear and compelling, creating both unity and urgency. For the Corinthians, it was all about unity as the Body of Christ. For the Ephesians, the body image comes back but with an emphasis on growing in health and strength. For the

Colossians, the vision is Christ as the unifying factor under which everything else finds its place. For the Philippians, the vision is one of friends and partners joining with the mind and style of Christ Jesus. Finally, we have Peter, who writes, "You also, like living stones, are being built into a spiritual house to be a holy priesthood, offering spiritual sacrifices acceptable to God through Jesus Christ.... You are a chosen people, a royal priesthood, a holy nation, God's special possession, that you may declare the praises of him who called you out of darkness into his wonderful light" (1 Peter 2:5, 9).

We could talk about Noah, Moses, Joshua and Caleb, Elisha, Nehemiah, Peter, Paul, John the Apostle, John the Baptist, and many others in the Bible who demonstrated great vision and interpreted reality with the eyes of God. We should trust that God has a divine purpose for our lives and our ministries. Our assignment is to discern this vision and take steps to make it reality.

Define the Vision

The first step is defining the vision that God gives. To do this, faithfully pray for the Lord to show you what he wants to develop in the congregation or ministry to which he has called you. Then take an inventory of your gifts, abilities, and interests and think about how you could put them into service for God. Remember that Scripture shows us God's purposes for the whole Church. The vision you will be defining is the particular expression of the way that God's purposes can be worked out in your local context and according to the gifts, passions, and personality that he has provided for you. The vision can be adjusted and changed according to the context—that is, the needs, challenges, and opportunities of the area of ministry— but it must always be rooted in God's purposes for his Church. For example, one of God's purposes for his Church is for it to praise and worship him. Music and songs are a part of that praise, but the style of the music and the instruments used, if any, reflect the values and general context of the local congregation.

A process that has worked for some groups is to gather the leaders of the congregation and spend a day discovering the hopes and dreams that God has put in each one's heart. A further step is to gain input more widely from the whole congregation so that everyone has a chance to speak into it. For this, you can use different tools, including the Strategic Planning Process tools provided free on the Multiplication Network's website (www.multiplicationnetwork.org).

Many churches are now facing disillusion with "Vision." One reason for this is that the vision development process often works perfectly. The vision clarified what was most important to the congregation and the direction they were going. The problem is that not everyone was in agreement with these choices. What some valued most perhaps was not included; they were either disappointed or outright angry and left to find another church that fit them better. The church became distraught over the broken relationships and loss of brothers and sisters in Christ. Unfortunately, this is often inevitable when setting vision. It is easy to paper over differences when you are content to sit where you are. Moving forward will require change and loss. The congregation should take this loss seriously. It should be taken seriously both because we are brothers and sisters in Christ and those bonds should never be severed lightly, but also because if the pain is too high, the congregation is likely to become paralyzed and refuse to risk change again in the future. Avoiding this scenario requires creating a vision-setting process that includes input from as many people as possible. Even if the decisions ultimately go the other way, people are more likely to stay and change if they know they had a voice in the decision. If nothing else, they are more likely to leave with fond regret rather than anger so that relationships are maintained. Inevitably, you will pay a price when pursuing a vision. Consciously or not, you will "choose who you lose" in the process because some people will not buy into the vision or participate in the process.

A firm and clear vision will correctly guide the leadership team and the new congregation and will foster the wise use of resources. It will also give direction to the church's other work areas. The persons responsible to steward the development of a vision for the community of faith are the leaders. They are the vision's crucial vehicle, the first ones to dream, the first to implement it, and the first in challenging others to see new horizons and to join the team to reach the stated goal of establishing a healthy church that gives witness to the gospel of Christ. Visionary leadership, rooted in Biblical values, will often end up in a Christ-centered church.

Share the Vision

You should share the vision that has been developed with others to seek confirmation by the wider community of faith. It is important to have people who are mature and wise within your community who confirm the vision God is giving you. Without their affirmation, it is too easy to put your words in God's mouth and pretend he was the one speaking all along. It is one thing to have your vision well defined in your head. It is quite another to communicate it clearly to others. To start, write the vision down and memorize it. Remember, the vision needs to be communicated in short, simple phrases that are easy to remember. If possible, use an image to accompany the ideas. You can motivate others by sharing the vision in a contagious way. To effectively communicate the vision and get other people excited about it, take the following steps:

A. Share the vision with clarity and conviction

You should communicate the vision clearly and with a sense of urgency. People will be more ready to work with you on common goals if they understand what the final objective is. The kind of vision that compels people is a clear, biblical, and achievable but challenging vision. Those who surround you will want to know what kind of ministry you are promoting, what your strategy will be, and where they will fit in that plan to make the vision a reality.

Some examples of a clearly defined vision:

To cross two or more cultural barriers: geo-political, ethnic, linguistic, worldview, socio-economic to plant indigenous churches and promote social justice. (**Xenos Christian Fellowship**)

To see the members of Cherry Hills be so passionate about God's heart for the lost that they become proficient in ministry skills and are pro-actively involved in strategic outreach ministries locally, nationally, and globally. (**Cherry Hills Community Church**)

Imagine a ragtag collection of surrendered and transformed people who love God and others. They are mesmerized by the idea that this is not about them but all about Jesus. They are transfixed by His story and His heart for their city. They are seed throwers and fire starters, hope peddlers and grace givers, risk takers and dreamers, young and old. They link arms with anyone who tells the story of Jesus. They empower the poor, strengthen the weak, embrace the outcast, seek the lost. They serve together, play together, worship together, live life together. Their city will change because God sent them.
They are us. (**unknown**)

We envision our church as joyfully celebrating a wide spectrum of opportunities for creating interconnections between Christ, our congregation, and our community, especially among those who have not traditionally connected with the church. Our central connection is with Christ, who invites all into covenant relationship and calls us to discipleship.

We seek to connect people to ministries for all age levels, especially for youth and young adults. We seek to foster interconnections of spiritual friends, connecting people to people, honoring their current level of involvement in God's mission, and offering them the means of grace to deepen that involvement. We seek to connect people to a changing community, especially to the least among us, with whom we seek to learn what the Holy Spirit is calling us to do and be. **(Falmouth United Methodist)**

We see an active congregation reaching the unchurched with the good news of Jesus; equipping them with a faith that works in real life; sending them out to serve the world in the name of Christ. **(Faith Lutheran Church)**

We see a church so in love with Christ that they are no longer comfortable with the fleeting American Dream; rather they are gripped by a vision to fulfill the Great Commission.
We see a church passionate for the nations, living and giving generously to fulfill the Great Commission.
We see our own sons and daughters going to the ends of the earth as short-term and career missionaries.
We see every member of our church empowered to fulfill a personal life mission in the world. **(unknown)**

New Life Christian Church will reach the lost people of Ciudad Juárez, disciple the chosen, serve the community, show Christian fellowship, and worship God in all aspects of life for the honor and glory of his name. **(New Life Christian Church)**

Exercise: Each of the vision statements above was designed for a unique congregation. Rate each one on its ability to unite and create urgency. How would you rework them to make them clearer and more compelling?

B. *Create an environment in which others can identify and participate in the vision*

There are people who have a tremendous vision for ministry but who do not let others take ownership of the vision. A true vision is a shared vision. People will not join in the vision if they cannot participate in creating it and executing the vision. This requires a careful balance. The vision must be firm enough not to change every time someone new joins the team. However, it must also be soft enough that every member can leave his or her fingerprints on it—if not in the vision itself, then in its implementation. People can take ownership only if they invest something of themselves in the fine print of how the vision works out in real life. We knew a church whose leader was a great visionary and who communicated the vision clearly. Nevertheless, he was not able to create an environment in which other leaders could participate in making the vision a reality. One leader after another passed through the church, but they were always sitting on the sidelines unable to invest themselves in a vision they weren't allowed to touch. The church never prospered.

To foster the vision, there should be an atmosphere of clear communication, transparency, honesty, respect, participation, and unity. Creating this kind of atmosphere is challenging because we as Christians tend to get passionate about our faith and defensive if any part of it is threatened. Open discussion requires humility, inviting disagreement, and having frank conversations without taking offense. It puts more focus on listening to someone else's heart than explaining one's own. In one congregation, the leaders have a simple tool for encouraging this, for example, at leadership meetings. They shake hands twice at each meeting, once at the beginning and once at the end. The one at the beginning is a simple greeting. After a heated discussion, the one at the end can be more challenging, but it compels them to set aside anger and embrace each other as one in Christ. Knowing that one is required to heal the rift before leaving the meeting helps one be more proactive in preventing it in the first place.

C. *Foster a team held together by the vision*

Every day we become more aware of the importance of working as a team. The ministry work of the church looks a lot like a soccer team. The players have a captain and a coach but if, during the game, they don't have a common strategy or no one passes the ball, they will not score the goal they desire. In ministry a common vision, guided by God, is the unifying factor.

A common vision can be the glue that holds a team together and moves them to accomplish great things. The Apostle Paul, for example, often traveled with another person. Scripture reveals that he did not always agree with his coworkers on all things, and he even had some serious conflicts with some of them, but they continued working as a team. It is evident that the gospel spread because people worked together and not just as individuals.

Our Lord Jesus Christ brought together the twelve disciples and with this group revolutionized the world around his vision for the Kingdom of God. He sent out his disciples to preach the gospel in teams of two. In the church today we should also work as teams and not as lone rangers. The common vision, centered on the person of Jesus Christ, will be the unifying factor for the team.

D. Allow for experimentation and failure

For the vision to become a reality, it may be necessary to try several strategies. There should be a place for new ideas, and there should be openness to the possibility that some initiatives will fail. Other people will be more willing to join with the vision if they know they have the freedom to fail when working for the desired goal. The famous inventor Thomas Edison failed thousands of times before inventing the electric light bulb we enjoy today. Other leaders will take action if you create an environment that allows for experimentation and some failure – in the end, you also could be more effective!

E. Keep the vision in everyone's sight

Churches should use all means possible to communicate the vision: preaching, teaching, literature, signs, banners, pamphlets, etc. Remind the congregation and the leaders regularly about the vision. Always look for new and fresh ways to keep the vision in front of the people who are involved.

> **Pastor Raúl has a banner in the sanctuary that says:**
>
> *Our vision is to become a congregation that grows holistically and that is dynamic in its function, Pentecostal in spirit, Reformed in doctrine and practice, and global in its reach. We see a community that is transformed by the gospel. This community worships God, loves others and works for Christ in his reign over all creation making all things new.*

F. Develop a concrete plan ("Put feet on the vision")

The vision must eventually have an operational plan that becomes the blueprint for making it a reality. Too many visions stay as dreams and are never put into practical action. Healthy churches will discover their clear and compelling vision, understand their mission, clarify their values, and convert all this into a practical operational plan supported by the available local resources.

A common reason for "Vision burnout" is that the congregation has spent countless hours developing a vision statement only to see it fade from view and sit on a shelf collecting dust. It becomes not only meaningless but a reminder of failed hopes and dreams. They have no desire to go down that road again. To avoid this scenario, it is important not to stop with a simple statement that captures the hope and dream for the future. Flesh it out into a concrete plan with a limited number of priorities (we often suggest just two) for the next two years. Within those priorities, set the mile markers that will remind you that you are making progress. Andy Stanley, Lane Jones, and Reggie Joiner in *7 Practices of Effective*

Ministry explain the first practice as "Define the Win."[5] He uses the sports illustration of scoring and seeing the numbers go up on the scoreboard. How will your church know that it is making progress toward the vision? Make it as concrete as possible and celebrate it.

Now that we have discussed the importance of a clear and inspiring vision, we can turn to those who are supposed to formulate and communicate it—mobilizing leaders.

"Even now, I beseech you, lift up the eye of
the mind: even now imagine..."
-Cyril of Jerusalem[6]-

A CLEAR AND COMPELLING VISION

Survey Questions

Mark the following survey on a scale of 1-10, 1 being a total disagreement, and 10 a total agreement. After finishing your evaluation of all seven phrases, add it up and divide by seven to get a general average for this vital sign. Then consider the questions below.

1. The church leadership gathers every year to evaluate the ministry and plan for the future.	
2. Our church has a clear and defined vision for a preferred future.	
3. Our church leadership knows where it wants to take the congregation two years from now.	
4. The pastor and the leaders communicate the vision clearly to the congregation.	
5. I feel inspired by the vision of the church.	
6. I know the vision and plan of the church.	
7. I feel a sense of enthusiasm over the future of our church.	

AVERAGE

For Discussion

1. What observations do you have regarding the results of the survey?

2. Which question made you think the most? Why?

3. What one simple step can you take to strengthen this vital sign?

Second Key Commitment
MOBILIZING LEADERSHIP

Leaders are those who understand and embody the vision, who communicate that vision clearly to the congregation, and who organize the body so the vision becomes reality.

Leadership is the essential link between the vision and the mobilized church body. A chain is as strong as its weakest link, but the leadership link should be one of the most trustworthy components in the entire ministry. The church needs leaders to communicate a clear vision and to formulate pertinent strategies. Administrators are necessary in every organization, and they contribute a lot, but one of the problems in many churches is that they settle for having an administrator at the helm and not a leader. What a blessing it is when the church has a leader with gifts of administration! But it can be frustrating when the person in charge is an administrator without the gifts of leadership.

A Definition of Leadership

In *Planting Growing Churches for the 21st Century: A Comprehensive Guide for New Churches and Those Desiring Renewal,* Aubrey Malphurs defines Christian leaders as "people committed to God (character), who know where they are going (vision) and who have followers (influence).[7]

First of all, Malphurs suggests church leaders should examine their personal character by studying 1 Thessalonians 2:2-12, where Paul highlights the characteristics of authenticity, integrity, perseverance, pure motives, justice, holiness, honesty, good conduct, tenderness, and friendliness. Malphurs agrees with Dallas Willard, who advises leaders to care for themselves with disciplines of abstinence (solitude, silence, and sacrifice) and action (confession, celebration, study, and submission). Much of the future health of the congregation will be rooted in the spiritual health of the leaders who plant it. Consciously or unconsciously, a congregation tends to inherit the spiritual DNA of its founding leaders, both their strengths and their flaws. Grace or legalism, hospitality or contentiousness, willing service or jockeying for position will flow less from official statements than from what is witnessed in the behavior of those who lead. Even the options between two healthy but different approaches such as bold faith and slow deliberative wisdom are more caught than taught. Character is key.

At the same time, mature leaders must have a clear personal vision. A Christian leader's personal vision should have its grounding in a thorough understanding of how God works in the world to expand his mission. Consequently, a Christian leader's personal vision must reflect how the leader understands God's calling and preparation for the leader to make a unique contribution to God's work in the present generation. The vision God grants to a genuinely spiritual leader is a vision of how he or she fits into God's vision for the Church and for the world. As Robert Clinton points out in *The Making of a Leader*, the task of a Christian leader is to help a specific group of people fulfill God's purposes.[8] With this in mind, the leader of God's people does not impose a personal vision on the group of God's people that he or she leads. Using a clear vision of how God is at work in the church and in the world, this leader guides God's people to discover how God wants them to make their unique contribution to fulfill the purposes of his Kingdom.

Church planters have the advantage of being able to begin a new entity that reflects their personal vision (i.e what God wants to accomplish in a church planting effort). As they develop a team of leaders around them, it is essential to make sure new leaders share the vision with those already on the team. Divided vision leads to tensions within the church: at the least, competing agendas, gossip, and minor conflicts and at the worst, a church split. Realistically, such tensions are a part of leading any group. Nevertheless, guarding and communicating vision on the front end can minimize these tensions.

Christian leaders need influence: their leadership will go only as far as their influence takes them. While a number of different elements factor into a leader's ability to influence, the two key factors are a relationship of trust and the sense of purpose. If people know a leader cares about them and has their best interests at heart, they will dare to follow. The Christian leader usually earns trust through the hard work of pastoral care. The sense of purpose in the congregation is often in response to the leader's passion for God, God's kingdom, and God's mission.

A large variety of literature on Christian leadership is available. Today there is broad recognition that different types of leaders function better in different situations. Here we identify the principal characteristics that those studying church growth and church planting have determined to be essential for the work of leadership in the Church of Jesus Christ.

A. Biblical Characteristics

Throughout Scripture, God reveals the characteristics of godly leaders. One key passage on leadership is found in Ephesians 4:11-16:

> It was he who gave some to be apostles, some to be prophets, some to be evangelists, and some to be pastors and teachers, to prepare God's people for works of service, so that the Body of Christ may be built up until we all reach unity in the faith and in the knowledge of the Son of God and become mature, attaining to

the whole measure of the fullness of Christ. Then we will no longer be infants, tossed back and forth by the waves, and blown here and there by every wind of teaching and by the cunning and craftiness of men in their deceitful scheming. Instead, speaking the truth in love, we will in all things grow up into him who is the Head, that is, Christ. From him the whole body, joined and held together by every supporting ligament, grows and builds itself up in love, as each part does its work.

In this passage, there is a lot to chew on. It describes a number of different leadership roles, all of them set up by Christ himself. Whether an apostle, prophet, evangelist, pastor, or teacher, every leader should have the same biblical goal: *to perfect the saints for the work of ministry*. In other words, the ENTIRE congregation and all God's people, not just the leaders, do God's ministry.

The leadership's function is to help the congregation find its place, with each member carrying out work corresponding to his or her gifts and talents. All gifts are for the edification of the body. Paul urges us to grow in everything, always centered in Christ. For this purpose, God enlists leaders who can direct the task and work of the church.

The most explicit epistles about leadership in the church are 1 and 2 Timothy and the letter to Titus. We list here some of the qualities necessary for elders or deacons in the church.

Description of the office of overseer or elder

Here is a trustworthy saying: If anyone sets his heart on being an overseer, he desires a noble task. Now the overseer must be above reproach, the husband of but one wife, temperate, self- controlled, respectable, hospitable, able to teach, not given to drunkenness, not violent but gentle, not quarrelsome, not a lover of money.

He must manage his own family well and see that his children obey him with proper respect. (If anyone does not know how to manage his own family, how can he take care of God's church?) He must not be a recent convert, or he may become conceited and fall under the same judgment as the devil. He must also have a good reputation with outsiders, so that he will not fall into disgrace and into the devil's trap (1 Timothy 3:1-7).

Description of the office of deacon

Deacons, likewise, are to be men worthy of respect, sincere, not indulging in much wine, and not pursing dishonest gain. They must keep hold of the deep truths of the faith with a clear conscience. They must first be tested; and then if there is nothing against them, let them serve as deacons. In the same way their wives [or deaconesses] are to be women worthy of respect, not malicious talkers but temperate and trustworthy in everything. A deacon must be the husband of but one wife and must manage his children and his household well. Those who have served well gain an excellent standing and great assurance in their faith in Christ Jesus (1 Timothy 3:8-13).

According to these passages, it is clear the testimony of Christian leaders is extremely important. A leader should use the Word of God well and study it; should be a person of prayer, humble, disciplined, and patient; should have integrity; and should be strongly committed to the Lord and his Church. Churches must be very careful when choosing leaders and should avoid selecting those who exhibit problem behaviors or negative attitudes.

Let's look at other biblical descriptions that apply to different roles of church leaders.

For this reason I remind you to fan into flame the gift of God, which is in you through the laying on of my hands. For God did not give us a spirit of timidity, but a spirit of power, of love and of self-discipline. So do not be ashamed to testify about our Lord, or ashamed of me his prisoner. But join with me in suffering for the gospel, by the power of God, who has saved us and called us to a holy life—not because of anything we have done but because of his own purpose and grace (2 Timothy 1:6-9).

Do your best to present yourself to God as one approved, a workman who does not need to be ashamed and who correctly handles the word of truth (2 Timothy 2:15).

Flee the evil desires of youth, and pursue righteousness, faith, love and peace, along with those who call on the Lord out of a pure heart (2 Timothy 2:22).

Preach the Word; be prepared in season and out of season; correct, rebuke and encourage—with great patience and careful instruction (2 Timothy 4:2).

But you, keep your head in all situations, endure hardship, do the work of an evangelist, discharge all the duties of your ministry (2 Timothy 4:5).

Similarly, encourage the young men to be self-controlled. In everything set them an example by doing what is good. In your teaching show integrity, seriousness and soundness of speech that cannot be condemned, so that those who oppose you may be ashamed because they have nothing bad to say about us (Titus 2:6).

Jesus as the example

Jesus was the Son of God who became flesh. He possessed all the gifts of the Spirit. What Jesus did individually, the church lives out corporately through the complementary gifts of the leaders and the congregation. Jesus models leadership for us. The Holy Spirit anointed and prepared Jesus for ministry. He also washed the feet of the disciples and said that he came to serve and not to be served (John 13:1-17). He taught with authority that being a leader is to serve. He led with humility. Whoever wanted to be first among the disciples was to be the last. Whoever wanted to be greater was first to be the least.

While our leadership styles may vary depending on the situation, our character should be shaped by the character and the person of our Lord Jesus Christ. We should always ask ourselves: "What would Jesus do?" or "What would Jesus want me to do?" After all, he is our supreme leader.

Henri Nouwen, in *In the Name of Jesus*, asserted,

> The Christian leader thinks, speaks, and acts in the name of Jesus, who came to free humanity from the power of death and open the way to eternal life. To be such a leader, it is essential to be able to discern from moment to moment how God acts in human history and how personal, communal, national, and international events that occur during our lives can make us more and more sensitive to the ways in which we are led to the cross and through the cross to the resurrection.[9]

Here we must touch on a typically neglected aspect of Christian leadership: Christian leadership takes us to the cross, through suffering, to the resurrection. Christian leadership is rooted in the leadership of Christ.

Robert Quinn, in *Change the World: How Ordinary People Can Accomplish Extraordinary Results,* wrote,

> Here's a heretical thought. Leadership is not about results. It is about commitment.... Leadership authors do not understand that leadership means "Go forth to die." If they did understand it, they would not be enticed to write about it – because people do not want to hear this message. Most people want to be told how to get extraordinary results with minimum risk. They want to know how to get out-of-the-box results with in-the-box courage . . . . The successful person got the result he or she desired because that person went forth to die . . . . The transformational result emerges when commitment meets resistance.[10]

While much is made of Jesus' model of servant leadership, the ultimate expression of that servant service - death on the cross – rarely appears in popular teachings on Christian leadership. Most popular teaching on Christian leadership minimizes the role of suffering in the experience of Christian leadership. However, J. Oswald Sanders, in *Spiritual Leadership*, observed, "Serving and suffering are paired in the teaching and life of our Lord. One does not come without the other."[11]

The Apostle Paul conveys this normal expectation of service and suffering for all Christians vividly in these words to church at Philippi:

> Your attitude should be the same as that of Christ Jesus,
> Who being in very nature God, did not consider equality
> with God something to be grasped, but made himself
> nothing, taking the very nature of a servant, and being
> made in human likeness. And being found in appearance
> as a man, he humbled himself and became obedient
> to death – even death on a cross! (Philippians 2: 5-8)

Likewise, Paul understood that serving in the power of the Christ's resurrection meant sharing the fellowship of Christ's sufferings (Philippians 3:10). This does not mean the Christian leader seeks to suffer or wants to die as a martyr. It does mean the Christian leader understands the greatest results often come when commitment to Christ, commitment to Christ's people, and commitment to the purposes of the Kingdom meet overwhelming opposition, difficulties, or involves personal risk. It also means the Christian leader is confident in hope that on the other side of the cross (opposition, difficulties, risk), there is resurrection (fulfillment of God's purposes). There is no crown without a cross.

What distinguishes Christian leadership from worldly leadership is the foundation of service to others that is willing to embrace suffering in order to fulfill the purposes of God. The shepherd gives his life for his sheep. Leaders serve at the same time they direct and guide. The spirit of service confirms a leader is a servant of the Lord. The servant doesn't command, dictate, or impose. The servant serves. Today more than ever we need service-based leadership. This is rooted in God's value of sacrificial love to the benefit of others.

Jesus as the commissioner

We can add to the above fact that Jesus Christ now reigns through his Word and his Spirit from his throne, and he himself sets up earthly leaders in his Church to prepare the saints for ministry

(Ephesians 4). Jesus is not just an example; he is the commissioner and sender. The last words of our Lord in Acts 1:8 were, "But you will receive power when the Holy Spirit comes on you; and you will be my witnesses in Jerusalem, and in all Judea and Samaria, and to the ends of the earth." He gives us power, and he commissions us for this task.

The fact that Jesus is our commissioner gives the Christian leader the tremendous assurance of knowing he or she is not alone. Church planters commissioned for the task of starting a new church have God's backing. This also gives leaders a large sense of responsibility, since they know that one day they will have to give account to their Lord and answer for what they did or did not do.

The leader and the grace of God

At this stage in the description of a Christian leader, more than one person will ask, "How can I develop all of these qualities needed to be a good leader?" Recognize that this is a process, part of the larger work of sanctification going on in each of our lives.

Christian leadership requires personal time with God, offering him the opportunity to do his work. Our study of Scripture and time in prayer ought to include some time to be agenda free – not focused on preparing the next sermon or solving the next problem. We need time with God designed simply to be with him, letting him teach and shape us. We can end our personal prayer time with 5 minutes of silence, holding back our incessant need to speak to give God the opportunity to speak to us.

In addition, we need to have the humility to let others speak into our lives. First, we should listen to people of wise counsel who we trust. As the writer of Proverbs puts it, "Wounds from a friend can be trusted (27:6)." Yet even our critics may have a truth we need to hear if we are willing to listen. In an effort to guard our hearts, it is easy to shut out those who might disagree with us. It is essential to sift through the chaff to find the kernels of wheat. They will help us hone both our character and our plans. Third, it is especially vital to listen to the leadership team that surrounds us. If those who share our vision raise a cautionary flag, it is time to step back and listen carefully to what God may teach us through them.

Robert Clinton examines the process by which God shapes leaders in Scripture from Moses to David to Peter and Paul.[12] There are some variations, but in every case, there were at least two checkpoints on the way: an obedience check where God asks the leader to take a large step of faith and a submission check, where God pauses to see if a leader will submit to authority even when the leader is convinced he knows better. Forward progress goes on hold until a leader passes both those tests.

Lastly, leaders should remember that character development is not just an exercise in self-discipline. The qualities we desire are fruit of the Spirit, which we can cultivate, but he must grow. The fruit is developed together in community. We should not rely on our own strength but rather on the grace of God. We hold on to God's promise to the Apostle Paul: "My grace is sufficient for you" (2 Corinthians 12:9).

B. Missional characteristics

After vision, leadership is one of the most important factors in any church, given that it transmits the vision and carries it forward. Leadership is part of the jar of clay that carries the treasure of the gospel (2 Corinthians 4:7). Mobilizing leaders must be missional— they must be leaders who see the world through the eyes of the triune God; leaders who seek to participate in God's mission in the world; leaders who call sinners with the Word of God and the power of the Holy Spirit. These leaders know their gifts and find others with complementary gifts to develop a more holistic ministry. It is helpful to note three key aspects of missional leadership.

1. **The church engaging the world.** Our communities are mission fields and the locus of God's redemptive and transformative activity! The most effective ministries are those in which the leaders do not only feed the sheep in the sheep pen but are also concerned, just as Jesus is, for the lost or missing sheep. This characteristic is essential in planting new churches and should not be lost in established ones. In Mark 2, we observe that Jesus calls Levi, a tax collector for the Roman Empire. Later Jesus went to have dinner with many tax collectors and sinners. When the scribes and Pharisees saw it, they asked the disciples why Jesus was doing this. "On hearing this, Jesus said to them, 'It is not the healthy who need a doctor, but the sick. I have not come to call the righteous, but sinners'" (Mark2:17). Biblical leaders focus part of their work on the needs of the community and include those who have never known Jesus Christ as their Lord and Savior.

    Kennon L. Callahan, in *Effective Church Leadership*, challenges the church to think less in terms of professional directors and more about missional leaders.[13] According to Callahan, we live in a time in which people are not seeking the church. Now leaders must prepare their congregations to go out and join the Spirit in what he is doing in the world. Leaders no longer have the luxury of simply being professionals who serve within the four walls of the church building and wait for those with spiritual needs to come seeking aid; rather, they must focus on the world, where God is reconciling people and the entire creation to himself.

2. **Motivating and involving the members**. A study of churches in Latin America by John Hall demonstrated that one of the most important characteristics of a leader is being able to motivate

and involve the congregation.[14] The traditional role of the "do-everything pastor" will rarely work in the postmodern context in which we live. Imagine the church as a bottle that is full of talent and potential for ministry. Leaders are the funnel that channels all of the talent and energy that comes from the bottle for the benefit of the Lord's work. Good leaders want to broaden, improve, channel, train, and delegate. However, there are other kinds of leaders, like the do-it-all pastor. This person does not allow the talents, gifts, and abilities of others to flow, but instead functions as an obstruction that causes the ministry to come to a standstill. This may be due to "leader worship," jealousy, fear, insecurity, pride, and other reasons. Today we need pastors and leaders who open new avenues of service and ministry for God's people and who do not stop the good initiatives that may emerge. Effective leaders are those who multiply themselves in others and who help all the members find their places in the ministries to which God has called them. Missional leaders help people see how every Christian is a missionary, salt and light, in their daily lifestyle.

3. **Seeding mission into every area of ministry.** God's mission has a church, therefore every dimension of church life needs to incorporate a focus on mission. In too many churches, programs cause a divided approach to ministry. There is one program for children, one for women, another for men, all focused on discipleship. There may be a program for counseling or for fellowship or for evangelism. Some churches even treat worship as a program of its own. This leads to a situation where everyone focuses intently on their specialty and leaves the other areas to their specialists. We intentionally need to cross-pollinate across areas of ministry. A missional focus should saturate all of a church's activities: worship, fellowship, counseling, finances, and all the church's systems. Every element of our communal life is about something bigger than we are.

Church-planting leaders clearly must have this missional characteristic. The challenge is to keep it alive once the church is established. Many movements begin with enthusiasm and vigor, but over time, they lose the vision and the spirit of sacrifice that they had in the beginning. They begin with a MOVEMENT full of initiative and missional spirit. Then they organize all of the aspects of the work to create a MACHINE, which, if well-oiled achieves even greater results while still conserving the initial spirit. At a certain point, formal structures can cause the organization to look inwards and to depend on the past, forming a spirit of traditionalism, or a MONUMENT. In this phase, the organization spends all of its resources on maintaining itself. In the end, as has happened with so many cathedrals in Europe, the organization ends up being a MUSEUM. May God cause many ministry projects to achieve the spirit of a movement and the organization of a machine, but may they avoid becoming monuments or museums. A missional focus is the key!

NATURAL PROGRESSION OF SOME INSTITUTIONS

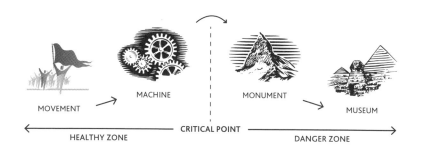

C. Differentiating characteristics

Recently there has been greater understanding of the variety of leaders needed for the diverse and complex ministry in God's work. The Lord uses different types of leaders in diverse places. Leaders are like fingerprints: no two are alike. However, just as fingerprints have certain general characteristics that aid in identification, there are different roles that leaders play. We have identified biblical and missional characteristics that a leader should have. What follows is a discussion of some of the wide variety of skills and abilities that are useful to greater or lesser degrees, depending on the context.

Authors Shenk and Stutzman, in their book *Creating Communities of the Kingdom: New Testament Models of Church Planting,* describe four types of leaders.[15] One person may have several of these characteristics, but generally, one characteristic is most prominent.

1. **Catalyzer.** This leader works optimally when he or she must begin from nothing. These leaders almost never need others to motivate them to work; they motivate themselves to start projects and can be very effective in planting new churches for a denomination. These people are often extroverted and confident and have the necessary charisma to attract others and begin a group or a new ministry. When things grow too complex, these individuals need help organizing things because they do not pay much attention to details—they are big-picture people. Catalyzers grow frustrated when things grow to a size that requires more structure and organization. This frustration causes them to look for new challenges.

2. **Organizer.** This type of leader can take something that is in disorder and organize it to maximize its effectiveness. These leaders like the challenge that coordinating and promoting a complex system brings. They build a solid structure from what was once a pile of loose pieces. They enjoy the challenge to continue organizing and improving. Many church planters identify with this type; they are able to structure things with the gifts and spirit of a businessperson. Some people would call this leader a developer.

3. **Operator.** This type of person is excellent at maintaining a functioning organization. Operators maintain the course of the church as long as there are not drastic changes in the environment. The majority of leaders fall into this category, although they may share characteristics of other styles. Operators make limited use of the more entrepreneurial aspects of the other styles and the more visible leadership behaviors associated with those styles. Nevertheless, every established church needs the talents and gifts of people who know how to lead through administrative skills. Surprisingly, studies show that in the business world, the majority of the brightest and best paid leaders and managers fall into this category.

4. **Revitalizer.** This person has certain characteristics of the previous three categories that allow him or her to mobilize and "resuscitate" a church even when it is declining. These leaders have many qualities similar to the catalyzer, but they begin with something that has already been established, a situation that has both advantages and disadvantages. For example, one disadvantage includes having to retrain and motivate members of a church who are accustomed to not working. An obvious advantage is that they don't have to start from zero and often have some very capable people in the existing church. Revitalizers frequently have gone through a variety of experiences and can use the many lessons they've learned in the new context in which they find themselves.

Leadership Styles

The academic literature describes many leadership models. However, we will focus on three types of leaders that one often encounters. First are autocratic leaders, who are bossy and overbearing and who think they are indispensable. They believe others must follow their instructions without protesting or evaluating. At the other extreme are the easygoing leaders, who are soft or passive and allow people to do what they want. Everyone can voice an opinion, and decision-makers never reach a consensus. The group with this kind of leader feels that it has no direction or guide. In its extreme form, passive leadership is actually a lack of leadership. A third style of leadership is participative leadership.

Participative leaders involve other people in decision-making and take others' opinions and constructive criticism into account. They lead with flexibility and know how to discern when to assert their authority. They don't impose and are receptive to suggestions and improvements.

Good pastoral leadership discerns the best time to exercise one style over another. Studies in the field of church growth show that different styles function better in different situations. In many church environments, a participative, visionary, and directive style seems to function best. A strong, firm leadership style is common in many cultures, but in the church, leaders who are accustomed to this style should take into account the opinions of others, share power and authority, and base their leadership on serving others.

The following chart presents several sources of power and influence. It is important for leaders to be aware of the extent of their influence and their limitations and how these relate to their part in doing the mission of God.

Organizing the Leadership of the New Church

In the context of new communities of faith, every church planter faces the task of organizing the church's structure and leadership and determining how to exercise biblical discipline. In this case, those who are planting a church within a certain church governance structure that they know and appreciate have an advantage. The three most well-known styles of church government are the episcopal style, with a system of bishops; the Presbyterian style, with a system of elders and consistories; and the congregational style, with a system in which the final word rests with the congregation itself. Church planters who do not have a predefined system of church government would do well to study the New Testament carefully and meditate on how to apply the biblical truths to the cultural and political context in which they find themselves. The church's form of government should connect well to its function of carrying out God's purposes in a biblical and relevant manner in a particular culture.

We also recommend creating an organizing document or church constitution. These statements provide the basic parameters for the order and smooth operation of the congregation. Dr. David Hesselgrave provides a list of elements for a model document:

1. Purpose and goals
2. Functions of the leaders
3. Qualities and method for selection of the leaders
4. Process for decision-making
5. Parameters for membership
6. General doctrinal standards
7. Rules of conduct
8. Matters of discipline
9. Matters of finances
10. Matters of property
11. Requirements of the local government[16]

For a more detailed discussion on this topic, look for books on the related themes of biblical discipline in the church and church government.

So far, we have established the importance of a clear and defined vision. This vision does not exist in a vacuum. Men and women called by God to lead his people live the vision and communicate the vision. We've also considered some factors that will enable those leaders to mobilize and organize the ministering body.

"I did not come to be served, but to serve."
-Jesus Christ
(paraphrase)

MOBILIZING LEADERSHIP

Survey Questions

Mark the following survey on a scale of 1-10, 1 being a total disagreement, and 10 a total agreement. After finishing your evaluation of all seven phrases, add it up and divide by seven to get a general average for this vital sign. Then consider the questions below.

1. The leaders create opportunities for developing new leaders.	
2. There are leaders being trained and prepared for future positions of leadership.	
3. I feel the leadership circle of the church seeks to reproduce itself and grow.	
4. I can identify at least two new leaders who have been developed in the past year.	
5. The leaders help and guide those desiring to become active in the church.	
6. The quality of our leaders in the church is very good.	
7. The leaders are decisive in the direction they want to lead the church.	

AVERAGE

For Discussion

1. What observations do you have regarding the results of the survey?

2. Which question made you think the most? Why?

3. What one simple step can you take to strengthen this vital sign?

Third Key Commitment
MOTIVATED MINISTERING BODY

The members of the church work in unity, using their gifts to serve their congregation and the community.

The key commitment of a mobilizing leadership links vision to the element of a motivated ministering body. The effective leader knows how to motivate and involve the congregation and how to multiply the number of leaders in that congregation. This is the discipleship model in 2 Timothy 2:2, in which Paul instructs young Timothy: "And the things you have heard me say in the presence of many witnesses entrust to reliable men who will also be qualified to teach others." Having a leader who is inspiring and has charisma is a big advantage, but this is not the only model, as so many biblical examples of leaders show us. Paul's instructions to his disciple indicate that Timothy was likely quiet and shy. The Bible demonstrates that God frequently uses the person we least expect to do his greatest work. Nevertheless, charismatic or shy, the truth is none of us accomplishes God's purposes alone. God established the church as a community of believers so we could participate in God's mission together and learn to love each other in the process. Therefore it is essential to challenge the congregation to unite in reaching its established goals and objectives.

An effective leader delegates to others not just to get out from under the work, but above all because it allows others to use their gifts to minister to others as they grow in responsibility. You are not just growing "your" ministry. You are growing people. After all, it is God's ministry! We are only stewards in growing God's people.

There are leaders who do not want to delegate because they think others will not do a job as well as they themselves can, or because they think the quality of the work will not be adequate.

They are not willing to take the risk that a task may fall through the cracks. Nor do they want to take the time to teach someone else. In the short term, it is quicker to do the task yourself. Training takes time and energy. Still other leaders do not want to delegate because they think that others may do the work better than they can do it. Usually they are unwilling to say the words aloud, but they are threatened by feeling that someone else's success will make them look bad. These leaders let their pride and jealousy eclipse the ministry and the formation of leaders.

Moses, in Exodus 18, had to accept the advice of his father-in-law and stop doing everything by himself. Jethro recommended that Moses delegate most of the work to others so that he would decide only the most difficult cases. The entire nation benefited in a short while. In the same way, today's leader should include others when assigning tasks in the church's ministry. See the box "Contrasting Leadership Styles" below and ask yourself how this would impact the mobilization of the church body.

CONTRASTING LEADERSHIP STYLES

THE AUTHORITARIAN LEADER:	THE SERVANT LEADER:
Says: "Follow me!"	Says: "Let's follow Jesus!"
Decides what his vision and goals are for the church.	Works with leaders to discern the vision and goals God has for the church.
Doesn't delegate, just gives orders.	Involves others.
Makes decisions on his own	Invites others to participate in making decisions.
Complains about the weaknesses of the congregation.	Strengthens the congregation in its areas of weakness.
Does everything himself: preaching visiting, praying, teaching, leading worship, etc.	Trains others to do ministry and affirms them.
Sees other leaders as competitors and threats.	Sees others leaders as partners and blessings.

For new churches, some experts suggest that church planters should spend eighty percent of their time with twenty percent of their congregation—their key leaders—once a core group has been formed. These new leaders will shepherd and mobilize the rest of the emerging church. One of the reasons there are so many churches of between thirty and fifty people is that most of the work is left for the pastor to do alone. Thirty to fifty people is, in the majority of cases, the number of people that one person can pastor without much help. What is clear from experience is that the leader who is going to grow and expand the ministry must use and maximize the gifts of everyone in the congregation. In the book *The Pastor-Evangelist: Preacher, Model, and Mobilizer for Church Growth*, professor Roger Greenway teaches that the responsibility of the Christian leader includes not only preaching and teaching the gospel but also the mobilization of the congregation to participate in ministry. The church planter is obligated by his or her call to mobilize new believers and to give them space to grow and develop their gifts for the benefit of the new congregation in its mission in the world. The pastor can help connect new people to what the Spirit is doing in and through the congregation.[17]

One of us participated in a small group Bible study in which a colleague gave a small package to every person there. We did not know what it was, but it looked like a gift. "What should you do to find out what it is?" he asked. We answered that we had to open it, and we did. We were surprised when we realized each person had a piece of a puzzle in his or her hands. Then he asked, "What should we do for this to be useful?" At that moment, we understood what the leader wanted to teach. We had to work together if we wanted to see the completed puzzle. We moved to a table and worked together, putting the pieces of the puzzle in their places until we began to see a beautiful scene of a church in a field. But we noted that there were some pieces missing to finish the puzzle. "Raúl, there are pieces missing," we told him. He asked us to return to our seats and then he spoke to us, full of excitement: "Each one of us has been given a spiritual gift and talents. But it is of no use by itself. It is meant to fit with the gifts of others. And there are pieces that are missing. We have to seek more lives for Christ, and then the gifts of these new believers will complete the work that we have begun in this church. But the only way to do it is to work together!" What a great lesson we learned that day! It is only in the measure that each person discovers his or her gift, a gift from the Holy Spirit, and puts it to service in the community of faith in mission, that we can carry out God's purposes for his Church.

In reality, it does not always seem to work out this way. Although they don't say it, many believers' concepts of church are imprisoned within the four walls of the church building. There are too many inactive Christians in established congregations. They are not serving nor are they involved in ministries. When the members of the body are not enabled to find their places of service and ministry, we have the tremendous problem of unemployment in the community of faith. There are many consumers and few contributors. There are many reasons why this happens, but here we will mention two key factors: one related to the leader, and the other to the congregation.

The Leader and Congregational Unemployment

The first reason why such a large percentage of most congregations are "unemployed" in ministry is that many leaders foster an attitude of neglect, although they do not do it intentionally. Sometimes because they want to do it all, pastors do not make space for others to find their place in ministry. As mentioned above, while some leaders do not include others because they think others cannot do the work as well, other leaders don't let things go because they are afraid that others will do things better! It is very important for church leaders to set aside the feeling of being threatened, which can arise when it seems that others know how to do things better. If we are to overcome these feelings, it is vital to develop relationships of trust within the leadership team and to create an atmosphere of transparency and honesty. As we deepen our trust in the Triune God, we can deepen our trust in the leadership community that reflects the love and unity of God.

Often people are waiting to be invited privately, and they will never raise their hand in public to accept an assignment. Many leaders will help the kingdom if they approach more people in private to help them find their place in service and ministry. It is interesting to note that while the members of the congregation are responsible for using their gifts, the way the leaders work and what the leaders teach can solve many of the problems of "ministry unemployment."

The Congregation and "Ministry Unemployment"

The second factor is the congregation's responsibility. Sometimes a congregation grows accustomed to not working because they think that this is why they hired the pastor. People use the excuse: "That's what we pay the pastor to do." This happens more in established churches than in new ones, but it is important to teach and work against this erroneous concept from the start.

Church members certainly have many things that occupy their time, and they often use the excuse that they are too busy to participate in ministry. Others do not have enough confidence in themselves and assume that they are not qualified to be used for the good of the kingdom. Or they may think that they are not worthy to participate because of a past sin or failure. Still other members may have contributed to the work of the church in the past and now say that they already have done their part. Others may have had a bad experience and avoid service for fear of reliving that painful event. Others may have been placed in the wrong type of work and now do not want anything to do with service or ministry. That is why it is so important to place people in the functions that God has given them gifts and talents to do. It is important for people to have some level of satisfaction in their service.

Mission or Maintenance

Many of these problems of "unemployment" arise when people do not understand the church and its essence. The attitude of a church body that is not active in ministry is reflected especially by communities of faith that think of the church as the physical building where they meet. Church for them is a place one visits or an event one attends. Many believers think that when they go to the church building to worship God, they have completed their task and function as believers. They do not understand the concept of being the Church of Christ, and therefore they do not understand what they are called to do.

Other churches, once established, are simply too comfortable and satisfied with things the way they are. They are self-centered congregations. Their programs and budgets serve those who are "inside." These churches look at themselves in the mirror, but they do not look out the window to see and serve alongside their community and those who do not yet know the hope of Jesus Christ. When there is no mission with what the Spirit is already doing in the community, there are far fewer places to serve, and therefore there is less need to mobilize the entire congregation in ministry— with just a few people, things can move along. Some churches focus on mission and others on maintenance. The difference is enormous.

The Priesthood of All Believers

It is time for the whole church to be set free to minister. It is time to mobilize all of God's people in each local church to serve him with the gifts he has given them. This is essential because this is the nature of the Church of Christ! The body of a missionary God is a missionary church. When Christ established missionary mandates like the Great Commission, he was not speaking only to pastors and ministers, but to all his disciples throughout time. The principle of the priesthood of all believers, proclaimed in the letter to the Hebrews and restated during the Protestant Reformation of the sixteenth century, should be rescued and put into practice. As we've heard often: "Pastors don't give birth to sheep—only sheep give birth to sheep." Pastors care for the sheep and guide them. The church is most effective at fulfilling its calling when everyone is working for the same purpose.

Studies with Latino churches in the United States confirm this reality. Some surveys with congregations averaging between thirty and fifty people indicated that fifty-five percent of the people became part of the church through a friend or relative, while less than twenty-six percent came through the pastor. Other studies show that in large congregations, the difference is even greater. There is no doubt churches that teach and practice the priesthood of all believers, or "each member a minister," will achieve a much greater impact than those that depend solely on the pastor's abilities.

The graphic below is helpful to show that it is not just about "bringing people to church" but about mobilizing the church, God's people, to be salt and light in their community. Christians need to infect their culture with the Gospel not just when they are gathered but when they are scattered. As God's missionary people we are called to remember the "sent-ness" of the Church.

INTEGRATED PERSPECTIVE OF CHURCH

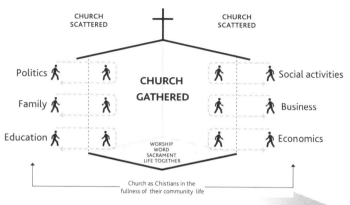

Adapted from Bryant L. Myers, *Walking with the Poor: Principles and Practices of Transformational Development* (Maryknoll, N.Y.: Orbis Books 1999), 133

Gift-Based Ministry

The Apostle Peter tells us in his first letter, "Each one should use whatever gift he has received to serve others, faithfully administering God's grace in its various forms" (1 Peter 4:10). Christians who do not use their gifts are, in general, bored believers because they are not doing the things the Lord created, equipped, and called them to do. And bored Christians are not good Christians! One characteristic of a Spirit-led church should be to have the highest possible percentage of members active in some ministry, based on their gifts. These will be vigorous and motivated members. Doing ministry motivates people. People become enthusiastic about their faith when they are doing things and learning things in the crucible of ministry and mission in and toward the world.

Researcher Christian Schwarz conducted an investigation that found very few factors were as closely relation to people's joy as to whether or not they were using their spiritual gifts. This study, carried out in over 10,000 churches across 32 countries, shows the importance of using the gifts of all members of the congregation.[18]

Helping people identify their spiritual gifts. Every year there are new materials available to help churches identify their members' gifts. Some publishers have workbooks with a study guide for leaders; we recommend some of the surveys that can be found online, such as the one found on the Multiplication Network site. Churches can help their members identify their gifts, perhaps by holding a weekend workshop, and can then place people in a ministry that fits them well. The key is for people to know their gifts and use them in a way that develops them further. Using their gifts helps people identify with the vision of the church, with its projects, and its programs. Note that our gifts are not only useful in a formal church program but also in our daily lives in whatever context the Lord has placed us. It is all used for His glory and points to His reign of a new creation in the world.

Helping people identify their passions. God has wired everyone differently. Three people with a gift for teaching may feel a pull to use that gift in different ways: one with children, one with seniors, another with individuals with special needs. Someone with a gift of evangelism may desire to reach those in prison or on the streets while someone else with the same gift has a burden for businessmen or mothers with small children. The difference can be discovered through a simple conversation or an informal interview with the church member. Often a God-given passion can be a stronger indicator where someone should serve than that person's gifts. When passions give the *where*, gifts will offer the *how*.

Listening to people's stories and helping them trace their history. God shapes us each uniquely for the task he would have us accomplish. Moses had to be a prince of Egypt to learn leadership skills and a shepherd in the wilderness to learn the countryside before he was prepared to represent God in the Exodus. David learned to trust God as a shepherd boy, military skills as an officer, and political skills in Saul's court long before he could assume the throne. God will use our life experiences, even those lessons learned in disobedience, to equip us for the tasks he has in store. Often it is at the point of intersection between our gifts, passions, and history that God intends us to serve.

Get moving. Identifying people's gifts and abilities and using them for the extension of the mission is part of God's model for his Church. It doesn't make sense if you identify a member's gift and then do not use it in ministry. The member will just grow frustrated.

Churches frequently face two roadblocks in mobilization. The first is not having a ready-made place to serve for each gift, particularly at a given maturity level. How much responsibility do you dare give a highly gifted individual who may or may not show up when needed? Often it requires partnering such individuals up with more experienced believers, ideally a team of believers, who can pick up the slack and also mentor them along the way. Create tasks to fit the individual and keep a list of opportunities that can be assigned at the spur of the moment. The other obstacle is not having training. If people are just thrown in the deep end of the pool and told to figure it out as they go, confusion and frustration is likely to ensue. At the very least, clarify the purpose of the assignment and some general parameters so that if they have to ad lib, members have a general direction to head towards. For example, for a greeter at worship services: "Make people feel welcome as if they were visiting your home. Let them know where everything is. Watch your attitude. They won't be glad they are here unless you are glad to be here." Provide as much training as possible.

Many people are not sure where their gifts lie, and many of those who already know their gifts are not using them for the building up of the church. This wastes one of the most powerful resources God has provided. We need to return to Ephesians 4:12, which commands us "to prepare God's people for works of service, so that the Body of Christ may be built up." Evidently, God wants his saints doing the work of ministry. That is why he gives gifts to everyone.

Missional Attitude

Another key factor is the attitude of the ministering body. This is measured in people's gestures, individual initiatives, shared smiles, and acts of service which, taken together, are more valuable than any individual program that the church has organized. This is a *missional attitude*—an attitude that stays focused on the presence of God's kingdom in our midst while seeking to imitate the mind of Christ, which goes against a culture that teaches us to put ourselves first.

One often hears phrases like "Members first!" Indeed, there are certain passages in the Bible that teach the priority of taking care of our brothers and sisters in Christ. But we also see in the Bible— from beginning to end—that God, in Christ, gives himself for us completely, we who once were lost. A missional attitude places guests and nonbelievers as a priority in order to give witness to the values of the Kingdom, such as sacrificial love to the benefit of others. A pastor once shared this situation that ocurred in his congregation. They were going on a trip to the beach, and more visitors came than they were expecting. There was not enough transportation. While they were trying to solve the problem, one woman exclaimed: "I'm getting on right now—members first!" This was the opposite of a missional attitude. Visitors who heard this would certainly think twice before joining a group of people with this kind of attitude.

Our attitudes reflect our values. If the missional aspect of the church is a core value of our congregations, it will be reflected in our actions. Having a loving attitude among the core members is worth more than having plenty of financial resources.

PRACTICAL STEPS

1. Prepare the leadership team to mobilize the congregation.
2. Teach about spiritual gifts and stewardship of talents.
3. Identify the gifts and the areas of interest of each believer.
4. Place each member in a role of service or ministry.
5. Monitor the whole system and make necessary adjustments.

Remember, it is better to first consider the capacities and talents of a believer, and then find a task for him or her that fits like a ring on a finger, than to write up job descriptions for the ministries and then try to find volunteers to fill them. In many cases, it is better to train people first and then get them involved, but sometimes you will have to reverse the order and get them involved first, training them little by little as you go. Ministry is the best motivation there is to continue learning. You should not assign people to ministries this way just because it is the most strategic way—although it is—but rather because it is part of God's design for your ministry.

Working as a Team

Part of mobilizing the ministering body also involves forming work teams, a core group, to produce more effective results. Developing a team is not easy—it takes time and effort—but in the long run, the investment is worth it.

Eight Characteristics of Successful Teamwork

Carl Larson and Frank LaFasto, in their book *Teamwork*, list the following characteristics of teams that work well[19]. They studied teams of all types: sports teams, mountain climbers, and teams from business, industry, and civil and government organizations. These eight characteristics emerged as the common denominator of all teams that achieved success. These characteristics are also necessary for those who work together in the context of the Church of our Lord.

1.	**A clear and inspiring goal.** When everyone works together toward a shared goal, the energy of the team increases and there is a common sense of purpose among team members.
2.	**A structure designed to get results.** The team should be organized in a way that aids in achieving the proposed results.
3.	**Competent team members.** A winning team always has competent members, people who know their responsibilities and their work well.
4.	**A shared commitment.** Each member of the team understands that sometimes individual preferences must be sacrificed for the good of the team.
5.	**A collaborative environment.** The team must promote good communication and a desire to collaborate with others.
6.	**A standard of excellence.** Efficient teams do not accept mediocre results. They work with criterion of excellence.
7.	**External support and recognition.** Teams that have the support and recognition of others tend to develop better objectives.
8.	**Principle-based leadership.** When the leadership makes its decisions based on principles, it gains confidence, the team functions better, and the team achieves its goals.

There is one pernicious and unhealthy practice that ruins teamwork and is worth mentioning here. Triangulation—when someone complains about one leader to another, without talking first to the leader with whom he or she has a problem—should be avoided. It is precisely the reason Jesus, in Matthew 18, made a priority of going directly to the person when there is a conflict. When someone approaches a leader with a criticism of someone else, the first question should be, "Have you talked to that person about it?" The second question should be, "Would you like to talk to that person together?" Triangulation in communication makes it difficult to form new leaders in the ministering body. It simultaneously erodes trust and deepens conflicts. Leaders should be trained to identify it and push back against it.

Bottom line, it is important for Christian leaders to realize that one of their principal functions is "to prepare God's people for works of service, so that the Body of Christ may be built up" (Ephesians 4:12). Healthy teams with healthy leaders can go a long way toward forming healthy churches.

A clear and compelling vision, given to mobilizing leadership that works with a motivated ministering body is given resources by God to achieve His ends in a given community. We now turn our attention to the proper stewardship of these resources.

"Use your ministry to build people, not the
people to build your ministry."
-J. Healey[20]-

MOTIVATED MINISTERING BODY

Survey Questions

Mark the following survey on a scale of 1-10, 1 being a total disagreement, and 10 a total agreement. After finishing your evaluation of all seven phrases, add it up and divide by seven to get a general average for this vital sign. Then consider the questions below.

1. The church helps members to discover their gifts for ministry.	
2. The church leadership trains members according to their gifts to serve.	
3. The church provides clear information to those who would like to serve in their area of giftedness.	
4. I feel the church has made it possible for me to use my gifts appropriately.	
5. I've been trained to serve or lead in the congregation and community.	
6. There are ample opportunities of service and ministry for those who wish to get involved.	
7. Our ministry structure is functional for mobilizing people into ministry.	

AVERAGE

For Discussion

1. What observations do you have regarding the results of the survey?

_____

_____

2. Which question made you think the most? Why?

_____

_____

3. What one simple step can you take to strengthen this vital sign?

_____

_____

Fourth Key Commitment
PROPER STEWARDSHIP OF RESOURCES

The church effectively challenges its members to be good stewards of their possessions, their resources, and their goods (their time, talent, and treasure). It uses these resources and financial donations to carry out the work of the kingdom of God in the church and in its community.

We have seen the importance of vision, leadership, and a ministering body for a healthy church. These three elements require resources to be successful. Thank God that when the Lord calls, he provides. God does not leave us to do the work without valuable and important resources.

We are not the owners of anything in God's Kingdom. We are simply stewards. God is the creator of heaven and earth and is the rightful owner of the entire cosmos. God has created human beings who carry the image of God to be stewards over all creation for the glory of God. Healthy congregations recognize the Cultural Mandate that God has given to human beings and understand the high calling this represents.

STEWARDSHIP OF RESOURCES

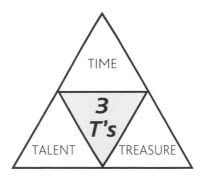

When we talk about resources, we almost always think about the three "T's": the time, talents, and treasure of the church, all of which belong to God. In the category of treasure, we include the church facilities, equipment, and finances. Every congregation, no matter how poor in finances or small in members, has some of each of these resources that God has provided for them to invest in the work of the kingdom. Many people begin by looking at a half-empty glass. But we need leaders of faith who see a glass that is half full and God's pitcher is still pouring! It is essential to remember that all of the silver and gold in the world belongs to God, and that where God calls us to work, he will provide the resources that are necessary and sufficient to fulfill his will. In the end, the whole world belongs to him (Psalm 24:1).

One of the principal mistakes of congregations in the area of finances is that people consider themselves the owners of what they have and not stewards of what God has entrusted to them. Even those who are committed to tithing can fall into the trap of thinking the 10% belongs to God and the other 90% belongs to them. An owner is emotionally tied to his or her belongings, while a steward simply takes care of and manages the money and property that belongs to another—in this case, no one less than God! It is the job of the leaders to model and teach a perspective on Christian stewardship to their congregations in a way that helps families to manage their finances and at the same time frees up resources for the work of the church in the world. The parable of the talents (Matthew 25:14-30) teaches us that when the Lord returns, he wants to find that we have been faithful with what he has given us, and he will hold us accountable for how we invested in the kingdom of God.

The second lesson we need to remember is that a growing church will always try to use its resources to the maximum. A missional church does not sit on money, but rather it is constantly using its resources to carry out God's work. A growing church is working at full capacity. It is possible that some projects will require saving, such as buying property or a future big project; it is also a good idea for a congregation to have a fund for emergencies. But the principal idea is to use the resources of the church to the maximum in order to keep doing the Lord's work. A missional church always needs more money, it always needs more workers, and it always needs more time. The church's management of its resources shows whether the church is really focusing on its community and its mission efforts. If a church says that evangelization is its priority but there is not a cent in the budget for it, then the church is only talking.

Let's take a further look now at the three T's in the specific life of a congregation:

A. Time

Time may be one of the least used resources for the Lord's work in most congregations. The time that members can use to serve in ministry to others is extremely valuable. It is the leaders' responsibility to challenge the members to get more involved and to mobilize them to use their time responsibly. Business people say that time is money, and they are right to some extent. But for the church, time represents opportunities to serve.

In one denominational study, the church members had an average of four hours per week that they could give to organized ministry. Imagine thirty people giving four hours per week—the congregation would have 120 hours for work and voluntary ministry every week! In different communities and cultures, the amount of time people have available will vary greatly. The central point, however, is clear: the church almost always fails to take advantage of the number of hours its members could give to serve as volunteers.

Church leaders should maximize their own use of time as well. They should invest time to mobilize the leaders they are forming as quickly as possible. The key is to identify the time that other people have available and to motivate them to use it for the work of ministry. Sometimes it is best to approach people in private, talk with them, challenge them to work in the ministry, and then place them based on their gifts and interests. As the work progresses, keep them motivated and make sure they are part of a work team.

Practical recommendations

1. Prepare a survey for the congregation, asking what times each member is available to volunteer during the week.
2. Collect the surveys and tabulate the results.
3. Analyze the results and compare them with the needs of the community.
4. Provide service and ministry opportunities for people according to their gifts, interests, and talents.
5. Have everyone meet with someone from the leadership team to coordinate the work.
6. Make sure the participants are informed and motivated. Hold team meetings once a month.
7. Ask for reports on the work to measure results and to celebrate victories.

B. Talents

Malphurs offers a delightful illustration of how not just time, but also the talents of many in the church are wasted. He tells how a football coach was giving a conference on the importance of being in good physical shape. A journalist interviewed him and asked him about the country's physical conditioning program. The journalist asked, "Sir, what would you say is professional football's contribution to the physical condition of the nation?" The coach replied, "Absolutely none." Surprised, the journalist asked him to expand on his answer. The famous coach responded, "Of course. I define professional football as 22 men on the field who desperately need to rest, and 50,000 people in the stadium who desperately need to exercise!"[21] Similarly, in the church there are a few people who seem to do all the work and a large majority who are merely spectators. Part of the solution is to find what talents are already present in the community of faith.

Some leaders do not have the slightest idea of the amount of "hidden" talents in their own congregations. If we could maximize the use of each member's talents, we would revolutionize the way we do things. It is a good idea to conduct a survey of the members periodically to create an inventory of the talents and abilities in the local church. This can be done by having each member fill out a card listing the things they like to do, the things they think they do well, and the talents they believe the Lord has given them.

You can ask the following questions of each member:

1. What gifts do you feel the Lord has given you to serve others?
2. What things do you like to do that others have confirmed you do well?
3. If the church were to help place you in a ministry, what would you prefer to do?
4. Would you be willing to take an inventory to discover your gifts?
5. When could we meet to talk about the results?

Some churches put a sign at the exit of the sanctuary that says: "Entry to the mission field." When the worship service ends and people begin leaving the room, they walk under this sign, which reminds them they are entering their place of work for the kingdom. People's gifts are not to be used just during the worship service, but in all aspects of life throughout the week.

C. Treasure (Location, Facilities, and Finances)

Location for new meeting places

Some scholars who have studied church planting stress the importance of the church's location so much that they say there are three factors to consider when beginning a new congregation, all beginning with the letter "L": (First, Location; second, Location; and third, Location).[22]

These days, in many places around the world, we have access to information about communities that we were unable to get before: the percentage of families that have vehicles and telephones, information on income levels, age, entertainment preferences, type of housing, etc. We can obtain this information from census data, from governmental agencies that work in urban planning, or from universities or financial institutions. In some countries, there are businesses that will provide this information at a modest price. It is worth doing a demographic study if you are thinking about the future impact of the congregation.

The decision about where to locate a meeting place is almost always made after studying the area and the people you hope to reach with the gospel. In rural areas people may want to attend the church that is closest in proximity, but in urban areas they may be more willing to travel to find a congregation that they like and where they may already know people. Some church planters have used valuable information regarding a large multifamily housing project that was going to be built in the area to help plan for the future.

However, Hesselgrave gives us something else to think about besides geographic location—the spiritual state of the area. He says that we need to seek a place where the Holy Spirit has been preparing people; otherwise, we may face years of frustration and little fruit.[23] In *Experiencing God*, Henry Blackaby describes the same factor another way when he says, "Find out where God is at work and join Him there."[24] That's not to say that God won't call us to challenging places, but jumping in where the Spirit is already moving definitely makes the work easier.

When the decision is to be made regarding where to locate the meeting place once the congregation has been established, it is important to look for a place with excellent visibility. Choosing a main street versus a small side street or a dead-end road can make all the difference in how many people will be able to find the meeting place. Visibility also has to do with having signs and with the first impression the place you have chosen gives to visitors.

Some communities of faith prefer a structure that stands out. Other contexts may require a building that looks like all the neighboring buildings, unlike the traditional idea of a church. This is why it is so important to first determine the needs and the customs of the people you are hoping to reach. Although it may not seem so, it is also important to know the reputation of the place that you may want to rent or buy. If a church moves into a location that has been used by different sects or pseudo- religious groups in the past, the community may never trust it.

It is essential to ask people who live in the community what they think about the location being considered.

Another important resource is the building or facilities that the congregation uses for its worship services and its church programs. Some congregations create a list of primary elements they need for their facilities. These include good lighting for evening activities, sufficient parking if people come in cars, a place that is adequate for teaching, good childcare, and clean bathrooms. A church in a rural area may not face the same expectations as one in the city, but it will have its own details to take care of to maximize the impression it makes on visitors.

Most consultants recommend expanding the meeting place once it is eighty percent full during worship services. Unfortunately, many churches that have not thought about having space to grow are faced with the need to change locations after a few months. And changing locations can transmit a feeling of instability to the community. A visionary church planter will invest the resources, even when it may cost a bit more, to find a place with enough capacity to carry out the programs that the church plans to develop and to allow for future growth.

Having said all this, we believe many Christians put too much of an emphasis on buildings, almost as if they truly believe God inhabited the building. Scripture is clear that the church is the people of God and that the Lord does not need a special edifice (See 2 Samuel 7:4-7). We see the desire for a building distracting many church planters from focusing on the task of building up the "living stones" where God truly inhabits—with His people. Many construction projects have sidetracked the Christian church into paying off large debts and channeling resources away from authentic mission. One of us once saw a leader showing a picture of a nicely built church building, freshly painted, and compared it to the dilapidated town clinic that was next door. He was proud in the comparison! One wonders where Jesus would have wanted the money invested. A better option, a missional one, would have been to first repair and paint the town clinic next door and later work on the meeting place.

Finances

The church, in practical terms, needs financial resources to achieve its goals of evangelization and bearing witness to God's kingdom. Without money, the church will have serious difficulties in doing the work to which it is called. The advantage we have is that when God sends us to do something, he also provides the tools we need to do the work.

Communicating Vision

Money almost always flows where there is a clear, motivating, and well-communicated vision. People are much more willing to donate their money when they participate in the work or at least see the fruit of the work. Giving to a general fund or to a denominational budget generates a lot less interest than giving to a specific project, like helping the young people raise funds for a community improvement initiative. Be as specific as possible when encouraging giving.

Transparent Accounting

It is the leaders' and the treasurer's responsibility to give a clear accounting for the income and expenses and to tell how this has contributed to a fuller participation in the mission of God. It is essential to give periodic reports to the congregation about the ways the money the church collects is being used. The finance department of the church should be managed in a way that inspires the trust and respect of the congregation. The pastor should be informed about the church's financial matters, but members who are knowledgeable in this area can also take care of the books, reports, deposits, and general movement of the money. Approval of payments, check writing, and reconciling can be done by different individuals. Two or more responsible deacons should count the offerings together. It is important for other members to take part in the financial control of the congregation. Some pastors think that placing their wife as the treasurer solves the problem, but this actually makes the ministry look like a family project rather than a church. Indeed, in many cases it creates suspicion that the church is being used as the pastor's private enterprise rather than the pastor serving the church. It is not our aim to discuss administrative details here, but the important point is that when people respect and trust the way the church's finances are managed, they are more willing to quickly and generously share their financial resources with the community of faith. Keep the church's finances transparent.

Teaching on Tithing and Stewardship

It is important for the church's leadership to lead by example in the matter of giving. Leaders should give offerings and tithes with thanksgiving and joy. Churches should teach Christian stewardship to all members as part of a discipleship program and as a required part of the new members' class. Scripture has much to say about money. It is part of responsible leadership to teach about the blessing of tithing and stewardship.

A healthy church will have a clear and inspiring vision that is communicated by the leadership as they mobilize the whole congregation into ministry. God provides the necessary resources which are stewarded appropriately as the fellowship of believers does its mission of pointing to the mission of God in its community context.

"A checkbook and financial statements are theological documents, they will tell you who and what you worship."
-Brian Kluth[25]-

PROPER STEWARDSHIP OF RESOURCES

Survey Questions

Mark the following survey on a scale of 1-10, 1 being a total disagreement, and 10 a total agreement. After finishing your evaluation of all seven phrases, add it up and divide by seven to get a general average for this vital sign. Then consider the questions below.

1. Our facilities are appropriate for carrying out our calling and ministry.	
2. Our church practices good stewardship in terms of handling the budget well.	
3. Most people give willingly of their time to serve the church and its ministry.	
4. Our church teaches regularly about stewardship and tithing.	
5. I feel personally motivated to contribute resources to the ministry of our church.	
6. The leaders keep the members sufficiently informed about the use of the church's finances.	
7. The congregation takes care of the pastor and its leaders.	

AVERAGE

For Discussion

1. What observations do you have regarding the results of the survey?

2. Which question made you think the most? Why?

3. What one simple step can you take to strengthen this vital sign?

Fifth Key Commitment
INTEGRATION OF TEXT AND CONTEXT

The church understands its context (the cultural, religious, economic, geographical and social aspects) and knows how to communicate God's Word in ways that make sense to the hearers.

The Centrality of the Text

The fifth commitment of a healthy church is that Scripture is taught and lived out in appropriate ways in the local and global community. First, let's look at how Scripture is central in the life of a congregation. Psalm 119:105 celebrates the wisdom of life based on God's instructions and has the oft-quoted verse, "Your word is a lamp unto my feet and a light for my path." A healthy congregation nourishes itself by reading and studying Scripture together. Apostle Paul wrote to Timothy, the young pastor of the church at Ephesus, "All Scripture is God-breathed and is useful for teaching, rebuking, correcting, and training in righteousness, so that the man of God may be thoroughly equipped for every good work" (II Timothy 3:16-17). In Colossians 3:16, he wrote, "Let the word of God dwell in you richly as you teach and admonish one another with all wisdom..."

This task requires that we spend focused time with God in God's Word and prayer, both as a community and also individually. So often the pressures of ministry compel leaders to use Scripture simply as a tool rather than as God's voice speaking into our lives. We will study the Bible to help us write the next sermon, prepare the next Bible study or minister to someone in crisis. We run from responsibility to responsibility until we are out of time, with the result that we are prepared just enough to explain the words to others but not enough to really listen and apply them to our own lives. In the midst of it all, we may assume that we have learned what

Scripture has to teach us, when in fact we have not taken the time to let God use it to shape us.

It is vital to church members to reserve corporate and personal time with God where we meditate on and pray over portions of Scripture that seem to yield no immediate ministry benefit. Often in those times, God will test our hearts and enlarge our understanding in ways we do not expect. When we set aside responsibilities just to be with him, our relationship with him has the opportunity to grow stronger and deeper. That depth of relationship will later feed ministry, but only if it is flowing from our affection for God. Using God or his Word as a natural resource to be mined to achieve our own agendas will simply deplete both our relationship with God and our ministry for him. A classic example of this comes in Joshua 9 when the Gibeonites seek a peace treaty with Israel. Joshua is so flush with success in crossing the Jordan, bringing down the walls of Jericho, and conquering Ai that he fails to take time to listen to God and falls right into their deception. God typically will only guide if we are ready to listen.

Time with God without a predetermined agenda offers the opportunity to let Scripture shape us when our natural tendency is to use our treasure chest of Scripture to pursue our personal goals. Well-intentioned leaders with a firm grasp of Scripture can easily pull out Biblical "trump cards" to cut off challenges and short-circuit arguments that need to be heard. The goal is always to let Scripture shape us rather than bending Scripture to fit our desires, no matter how noble those desires may be.

When that goal is personally pursued, it will also be reflected in the churches we serve. Each program and activity will be actively measured against Scripture. This is true not only in our activities but also our collective attitudes. Do we view people as God sees them?

Do we see his image in them, the impact of sin on their lives and our own, and Christ's heart for their and our redemption? Scripture offers us the glasses that help us see this world and the people in it through God's eyes. The vision of a church, while unique to that congregation, should always be gospel shaped.

Leaders of healthy congregations know Scripture well, they are shaped by it, and they apply biblical principles in their decision-making, handling of conflicts, strategic planning, evaluation of worship, and other aspects of church life. They read Scripture together and use it to nurture their life with God and to disciple church members. They study it, meditate on it, and memorize it. Scripture shapes the values of the congregation, and members use it to hold each other accountable.

Knowing the Context

Nevertheless, knowing Scripture isn't enough to enable a church to successfully reach its community. The church must also understand its cultural context in a variety of different dimensions: religious, socioeconomic, cultural, geographical, political, etc. This comes from listening to people, building relationships with them, living among them, and learning everything possible from and about them. As the congregation comes to understand people's motivations, problems, dreams, and values, it can meet its neighbors where they are and explain how the gospel addresses their deepest needs.

The graphic below helps explain how we can have initial interpretations about the context that can seem accurate, but are actually not helpful. Initial interpretations can be complemented by learning that allows new facts and perceptions to emerge so that the interpretation is refined over time.

THE CONFIGURATIONAL NATURE OF KNOWLEDGE

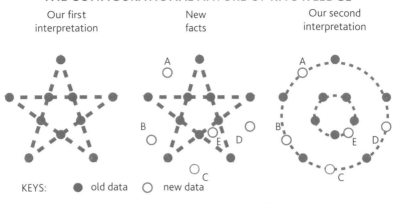

Our first interpretation   New facts   Our second interpretation

KEYS: ● old data ○ new data

Doctoral class with Paul Hiebert, Trinity Evangelical School 2002.

See also, *Understanding Folk Religion*, Hiebert et al; p. 41

A German-speaking congregation in a Spanish-speaking community would have a hard time communicating the gospel effectively to its neighbors—they speak different languages and have different ways of relating. But it's also possible that the longer we are Christians and the more time we spend with Christians, the more likely we are to create our own Christian subculture, with our own 'language' (expressions like 'getting saved' and 'Jesus is King,' 'born-again' and 'quiet time') and habits (praying together, going to church and Bible study meetings) to which people outside the church don't relate.

One theologian used to say we need to have the Scriptures in one hand and the newspaper in the other. To communicate the gospel well, we need to understand how our neighbors think and why they think that way. Then we can be ready to answer their questions about Jesus and our relationship with him, rather than giving answers to questions they aren't asking. When the Apostle Paul found himself in Athens, he went to a meeting of the Areopagus, where members would debate the latest religious and philosophical ideas. There he affirmed their interest in religion and used an altar dedicated to an "unknown God" as a way to introduce the gospel of the one true God: "Men of Athens! I see that in every way you are very religious. For as I walked around and looked carefully at your objects of worship, I even found an altar with this inscription: To an unknown God. Now what you worship as something unknown I am going to proclaim to you" (Acts 17:22-23). When Paul talked to the crowd in Jerusalem, he spoke to them in Aramaic, their native language, and started by introducing himself as "a Jew, born in Tarsus of Cilicia, but brought up in this city. Under Gamaliel I was thoroughly trained in the law of our fathers and was just as zealous for God as any of you are today...." (Acts. 22:3-4). When Paul spoke before the Sanhedrin, the council of Jewish leaders, in Acts 23, he mentioned his 'credentials' to them: "My brothers, I am a Pharisee, the son of a Pharisee. I stand on trial because of my hope in the resurrection of the dead" (Acts 23:6). In each case, Paul took into consideration who he was speaking to and the cultural context they were from. While the message of the gospel never changes, certain aspects of it connect more immediately with people in our community. As Paul knew, the strategies we use to communicate it should fit the people we are seeking to reach

Tim Keller, in *Center Church*, argues that contextualization is not telling people what they want to hear. "Rather it is giving people the Bible's *answers*, which they may not want to hear at all, *to questions about life* that people in their particular time and place are asking, in *language and forms* they can comprehend, and *through appeals and arguments* [that carry a] force they can feel, even if they reject them."[26]

One of the examples Keller offers from his context in Manhattan, New York, is a cultural allergy to the Christian concept of sin. As the American saying goes, "Rules are made to be broken." However, he found people resonated with the biblical concept of idolatry when it was presented as misplaced priorities. He often referred to

Augustine's description of sin in his Confessions as a disorder of love: "So, for example, if we love our own reputations more than the truth, it's likely we'll lie. Or if we love making money more than our family, we'll neglect our children for our career. Disordered love always leads to misery and breakdown. The only way to 'reorder' our loves is to love God supremely."[27] Depicting sin as misplaced love, not just a violation of the law, was much more compelling to the people he was trying to reach. It was still the Bible's answer (the Great Commandment) but to questions the people of Manhattan were asking (How do I maintain proper priorities in my life?) in a language they understood (business, family, priorities) with a force they could feel (even if they decided to put career first, they felt the pull of a better way).

When we contextualize, we walk a fine line between overadapting to the culture or underadapting to it. If we overadapt, the gospel begins to get watered down and we fail to issue the challenges that need be confronted in order for people to really wrestle with what it means to embrace and follow Christ. If we underadapt, people will simply turn away because, while they are hearing biblical truth, they are being given answers to questions they aren't asking in concepts that make no sense to them and with arguments that carry no weight in their world. We will have made the most relevant truths in human history sound totally irrelevant. We avoid the first error by continually going back to Scripture and making sure that the challenge to repent and believe has not been lost. We avoid the second by watching faces: Are they interested or bored? Intrigued or confused? Weighing what you say or waiting for you to quit talking?

Where to Start

Keller suggests contextualization is a three-step process: entering a culture, challenging the culture, and appealing to the listeners.[28] These steps overlap but remain distinct.

Entering a Culture

Entering a culture is all about immersing yourself in a culture to understand its worldview: the questions it asks, the things it values the most, the way it reasons and thinks and argues, along with its sources of hope and belief. Discovering these elements occurs on two different levels. One level is academic. What do the outside experts and academics see as the driving factors? Who are the movers, shakers, and trend setters? Where do they focus their attention? What are the subgroups of the culture? How do they interact and where do they conflict? Read the popular literature looking for themes and underlying assumptions. What are the popular styles of music and what is the focus of the lyrics? What gets discussed in the local newspapers and in the local coffee shops (or equivalent thereof)?

The second level is that of personal interaction. It requires spending hours and hours in close relationships with people, listening to them carefully. Ask questions. Invite feedback. Immersion into the lives of the people you hope to reach is vital. Not only will it field test the lessons learned from the academic study for accuracy, it will give those lessons flesh and bone so your awareness of the culture will become not only conscious but also intuitive.

There are a variety of valuable insights that will be gleaned by this two-level approach, but two should be targeted in particular. The first is the method of reason most commonly used. Hesselgrave in *Communicating Christ Cross-Culturally* describes three styles of reason. The first style is Conceptual (or "Western"), in which people reach decisions through the use of analysis and logic. The second style is Concrete Relational (or "Chinese"), in which people make decisions through relationships and practice. Decisions are shaped by the beliefs of the larger community and also by what the expected outcome will be for everyday life. The third style is Intuitional (or

"Indian"), where decisions are formed by insight and experience.[29] Stories and narrative have more influence than a well-reasoned argument. In truth, we are all more complex in our thinking than simply one style. Most individuals possess a blend of each though one may predominate. Yet the three styles offer a great starting point for understanding how cultures may overlap and be different at the same time. Understanding how people in a particular culture come to a decision is critical if what you hope to lead those in that culture to a commitment to follow Christ. Airtight logical arguments will be of little use when what a person needs is to hear the story of Jesus or to see an example of a Christ-shaped life.

HESSELGRAVE MODEL OF CONTEXTUAL DECISION MAKING

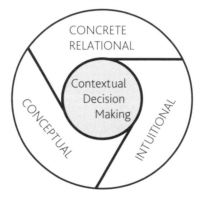

Adapted from *Communicating Christ Cross-Culturally.*

The second target of your research is the identification of the dominant worldview (or in some cases worldviews – plural). What is the central belief system and how do the parts fit together? Do they believe in a God, no god, many gods? How are right and wrong determined? Which behaviors/occupations/topics of discussion are honorable and which are taboo and why those particular examples? How do they view various subgroups: wealthy, poor, ethnic groups, women, children, those with disabilities?

Once you map out many of these beliefs and how they tie together, Keller advises that you divide them into two categories: A and B. "A" beliefs are those that, because of God's common grace, roughly correspond to biblical teaching. "B" beliefs are those that lead people to find Christian teaching either implausible or downright offensive. The key here is to recognize that what fits in the A category and what fits in B differs from culture to culture. Keller offers the example of Manhattan, where what the Bible says about turning the other cheek is welcomed (an A belief), but what it says about sexuality (a B belief) is resisted. However, in the Middle East we see the opposite. Turning the other cheek (a B belief) is rejected as unjust and impractical, while biblical prohibitions about sexuality (an A belief) make complete sense.[30] The distinction between A beliefs and B beliefs becomes important as we move to the second step of contextualization: challenging the culture.

Challenging the Culture

One of God's primary goals is to bring God's redemptive power to bear in working through the church to help transform whatever culture it is in by cultivating a worldview where God is king, Christ is at the center, and everything else finds it place in him (cf. Colossians 1). That requires the prophetic task of challenging the culture in which we live. There may be little need to challenge the A beliefs, but if we focus solely on the B beliefs in a direct challenge, we are not likely to create much change either. We are more likely to create walls of opposition. A healthier and more productive approach is to utilize the inconsistencies within a culture to expose its weaknesses. This is where the A beliefs prove to be so useful. Essentially you are saying, "If you believe 'A' about God – and you are right – then how can you believe 'B'? These two truths oppose each other." We start with premises from the Bible which they already agree with to point out where they have gone off track. Paul used this approach on Mars Hill (see Acts 17) when he argued from the little bit the Athenians understood about God to challenge them to believe in the one true God instead of idols. Jesus did the same with the Samaritan woman (see John 4) as he used bits and pieces of her limited religious understanding to lead her to the truth that he was the awaited Messiah.

The illustration mentioned above of Keller's approach to Manhattan's aversion to the Christian concept of sin offers a contemporary example. Sin is definitely a B belief (and not just for Manhattan). Rules and laws, right and wrong are frequently considered malleable, morphing at the whims of society. Idolatry, it turned out, was an A belief--not because people in Manhattan worship statues, but because they expend a great deal of effort setting priorities and could visualize the consequences of loving the wrong thing too much. Put in the terms of idolatry, they could begin to grasp the moral impact of their choices. Idolatry is sin, but sin in a form that challenges their Manhattan worldview.

Appealing to Listeners

The third step of contextualization is making an appeal to those who will listen in a manner they will find compelling. That is why it is so important to determine how particular cultures come to decisions during the "entering" step. The Bible is full of rich and diverse language and metaphors for explaining what God is up to: agricultural, herding, marital, familial, legal, political, economic. Sometimes God offers freedom from fear of judgment and death, freedom from slavery to sin and addiction, freedom from shame and guilt. Sometimes he offers to fill our deepest longings for purpose and meaning, for truth, for a place to belong. Sometimes Jesus offered answers, sometimes parables and riddles, and sometimes he asked questions for his audience to wrestle with. The goal is to tailor God's appeal in such a manner that it will not be casually dismissed but carefully pondered because his voice is evident. That way your hearers are not accepting or rejecting what you are saying. They are responding to him.

More than Words

Most of what we have said above has focused on the verbal aspects of communication. However, applying God's Word to a particular context is often just as much about what we do as what we say. Worship should also incorporate the best of the surrounding culture (music and art, for example) and use it for the glory of God. We are commanded by Scripture to praise God with voices and instruments. People in the Dominican Republic can praise God using instruments like maracas and güiras, people in Mexico can praise God using acoustic guitars and accordions, and people in Guatemala can praise God using the marimba. While it is wonderful to bring in a sense of the global nature of the people of God with instruments and musical styles from other places, let us never devalue the musical culture of the local community, but rather redeem it by redirecting it toward the glory of God.

The graphic below provides some of the options to be considered when contextualizing the gospel into a new setting. This has to do with the communication of the gospel but also with the doing of the gospel.

OPTIONS IN CONTEXTUALIZING CERTAIN CULTURAL BELIEFS AND HABITS

ACCEPT ADOPT	MODIFY CONVERT	CREATE NEW	REPLACE SUBSTITUTE	REJECT
Keep things that can be affirmed in the receptive culture	Give Christian meaning by reinterpreting some beliefs or recasting them in Biblical terms	Shape a new set of symbols, rituals, and language as the Gospel enters new cultures and subcultures	Take the existing ritual, holiday, or custom and replace it with a Christian one	Discard certain practices, rituals, language, etc. that comes in conflict with the Gospel and Christian values

Doctoral class with Paul Hiebert, Trinity Evangelical Divinity School, Feb 2002

The same principle applies to our lives both as individual Christians and local congregations. Our lives often speak with a volume that our words cannot match. The best example of this is the translation of the power of the Resurrection into the lives of the early church. Their faith in the reality of the physical Resurrection of Christ and their future life with him was so strong that they became living translations of the Easter story. In Acts 4, when the Apostles were threatened, they didn't tone down their preaching or even pray for God's protection. Instead they prayed for boldness, and when martyrdom came for so many, they faced it with a courage that made many of their captors start to ask questions. The willingness of Christians to care for others was put on dramatic public display when two great plagues swept the empire, one beginning in 165 AD and the second in 251 AD. Because of the lack of modern medicine, mortality rates climbed higher than 30 percent. Pagans tried to avoid all contact with the afflicted, often casting the still living into the gutters. Simply put, they were afraid. Christians, on the other hand, nursed the sick even though some believers died doing so. They did so because they were convinced that not even death would separate them from the love of Christ and the resurrection he had promised. The end result was the conversion of the majority of the Roman Empire in the space of 300 years.

As congregations "sink deep" both into God's Word and also into the community they are a part of, they become increasingly able to share biblical truth in actions and words that make sense to the community. Just as Jesus spent time in prayer but also went out into communities with the announcement of God's Kingdom (Matthew 4:23), we are called to spend time with God in order to be sent into the world (Matthew 28:18-20). In the book of Acts, the Holy Spirit–empowered people of God were to carry the gospel to Jerusalem (their immediate community), all Judea (their immediate region), Samaria (the neighboring, culturally different region), and the ends of the earth (Acts 1:8). Healthy churches will connect the text to the context being both faithful to Scripture and relevant to the culture in which they minister.

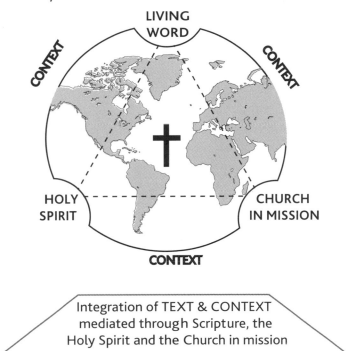

Integration of TEXT & CONTEXT
mediated through Scripture, the
Holy Spirit and the Church in mission

In this chapter, we've presented the five vital commitments for effective ministry. Now, with this foundation, we can transition to the next chapter, where we will discuss the five vital functions that have to be developed in a healthy church.

"I have become all things to all people so that by all possible means I might save some."
(1 Corinthians 9:20-22 NIV)
-Apostle Paul

Survey Questions

Mark the following survey on a scale of 1-10, 1 being a total disagreement, and 10 a total agreement. After finishing your evaluation of all seven phrases, add it up and divide by seven to get a general average for this vital sign. Then consider the questions below.

1. Leaders apply Kingdom values to the daily challenges in the community.	
2. The Word of God is the main guide for the leadership of the Church.	
3. It is evident the Word of God is used in the church's meetings and services.	
4. The Bible guides us in trying to resolve the problems in our community.	
5. Our church is aware of the needs in our social context.	
6. Our church tries hard to build relationships in the community.	
7. People see our church as a positive agent of change in our community.	
AVERAGE	

For Discussion

1. What observations do you have regarding the results of the survey?

2. Which question made you think the most? Why?

3. What one simple step can you take to strengthen this vital sign?

FIVE KEY FUNCTIONS
OF A HEALTHY CHURCH
PART II

The five indispensable functions upon which a healthy church is built are:

1. a compelling *witness* (the evangelistic function),
2. a comprehensive *discipleship,*
3. a compassionate *service,*
4. a caring and welcoming *community,*
5. a dynamic *worship and prayer.*

"Those who accepted his message were baptized, and about three thousand were added to their number that day. They devoted themselves to the apostles' teaching and to the fellowship, to the breaking of bread and to prayer. Everyone was filled with awe, and many wonders and miraculous signs were done by the apostles. All the believers were together and had everything in common. Selling their possessions and goods, they gave to anyone as he had need. Every day they continued to meet together in the temple courts. They broke bread in their homes and ate together with glad and sincere hearts, praising God and enjoying the favor of all the people. And the Lord added to their number daily those who were being saved." Acts 2:41-47

The Bible, from Genesis to Revelation, contains abundant evidence that God has a plan for his creation. But when we reflect on the function of the Church—God's central instrument for bearing witness to his kingdom and reign—we think of the Church that is described in this very familiar passage. On Pentecost, the Church receives power from on high to achieve God's purposes. God's Spirit is poured out on the Church so that it can carry out Christ's orders. This Church is dynamic, joyful, and enthusiastic; it is also obedient, suffering, and faithful to its Lord. But we only have to read the rest of the book to see that it also faces conflicts, false teachers, deceivers, jealousy, and pride. However, in Acts 2:41-47, the Church is seen in its first love, fulfilling the functions and purposes for which Christ established it. We remember that Christ himself said, "I will build my Church" (Matthew16:18). Jesus glorifies the Father by building his Church and extending his mission. In the following pages, we will identify the purposes of the Church in this passage from Acts 2 and suggest some ideas for healthy conversations in the local congregation.

First Function
COMPELLING WITNESS
(The Evangelistic Function)

The Church announces the good news of Jesus Christ in word and in deed and invites people to be a part of the Kingdom of God.

"And the Lord added to their number daily those who were being saved" (Acts 2:47).

God is the one who makes things grow. The Bible is clear about this. The disciples received the command to go and preach the gospel, but they understood that God, through the Holy Spirit, was the one who made the church grow. Three thousand people had just been added to the community of faith through Peter's sermon. God was blessing the New Testament church powerfully and quickly, spreading the gospel of Jesus Christ everywhere. Acts 16:5 affirms this: "So the churches were strengthened in the faith and grew daily in numbers."

We know that one plants and another waters, but God produces the growth. This rule continues today. Human beings plant and water, but God continues to be the one who makes things grow. Nevertheless, it is important for our churches to expect the growth that God can produce. The sad thing is that there are many congregations that have such low expectations that they always achieve them—they simply do not grow.

We need to trust the Lord will continue to call his chosen people and add them to his flock. The Church is the instrument that God uses to find the lost and to disciple the found. The Apostle Paul speaks often in his epistles of the elect whom God called before the foundation of the world (see Ephesians 1:4, for example). We do not know who the elect are, but we do know that God is working ahead of us to prepare them for his message. Therefore, we must proclaim the good news to the whole world to find those whom the Lord is calling. The Lord will add them to his flock, but he invites us to be his instruments in the search. We are compelled to obey the biblical imperative to go and make disciples of all nations.

The last command Christ gave us before he ascended into heaven should be our first priority. We cannot settle for merely a testimony of presence; rather, when and wherever possible, we have to verbally proclaim the good news of Jesus Christ. Jesus' initial invitation to his disciples affirms that he calls us for this purpose: "Come, follow me, and I will make you fishers of men" (Mark 1:17).

The New Testament uses derivations of the Greek word for witness (*martys*) more than two hundred times. One who testifies (*martyreo*) and gives his testimony (*martyrion*) fulfills the biblical command for all Christians (Luke 24:48 and Acts 1:8). It is interesting to note that the word "martyr," one who dies for a cause, is derived from *martyreo*. Giving testimony to the Lord Jesus Christ in many cases has meant suffering, discomfort, and even death. Some have said that the blood of the martyrs is the seed for new converts.

When we talk about evangelism in the context of church planting, people always ask, "What is the best method for evangelism? What produces the most results? What style should we use?" The truth is that there is no magic formula to solve all the evangelism challenges. The methods of evangelism are as endless as the opportunities before us: personal-relational evangelism, evangelism by telephone, outdoor evangelistic worship services, worship services in homes, evangelistic cell groups, concerts, preaching, and small groups. All of these have their time and place. One method may work well for one church, but when another church tries it out, it is a disaster.

Each local church should find a method that is appropriate to its context and put it into practice. There are too many conferences on this topic and too little implementation. A lady once criticized the evangelism methods used by Dwight L. Moody, the famed 19th century American pastor, to win people to saving faith in the Lord Jesus Christ. In response Moody replied, "I agree with you. I don't like the way I do it either. Tell me, how do you do it?" Moody's critic answered, "I don't do it." Moody quipped, "In that case, I like my way of doing it better than your way of not doing it."[31] *What is important is for the church to choose some way to evangelize and to practice this evangelism in a consistent fashion that is relevant to its community and faithful to the Gospel!*

Know the People You Hope to Reach

Getting to know the people you are hoping to reach happens on two levels. The first is in a more clinical, demographic way. Define the characteristics of your culture. Where is it at spiritually? Is it Christianized so that even if the members of your community aren't believers, they still have an awareness of God, respect Scripture, and treasure basic Judeo-Christian values? Is it a post-Christian secular community where notions of God are dismissed, truth is defined by science, and values are relativistic based on "what's working for me right now"? Does your community have Islamic, Hindu, Buddhist, or other religious roots? Is it an honor/shame culture or an individualistic one? What are its idols: family, success, fame, wealth, scientific truth, military strength, sexual prowess? Where do its mores diverge from Christian values? Who in society is valued and who is devalued? How are the vulnerable–women, children, poor, disabled, minority groups–treated?

At the same time, begin to build relationships with a variety of individuals with no agenda other than to get to know them and learn how they think and feel and live. What are their aspirations and fears? If God provides the opportunity to share your faith with them, by all means take it. However, the goal at this point is simply to listen and learn. Who are these people you are hoping to reach? These individuals will become a reality check for your observations on the general culture.

Identify a Niche Group

In the end, these observations, bathed in prayer, should lead to two discoveries. The first is whether there is a particular niche group in your community whom God is calling you to reach.

Prince of Peace Church, a church plant initiated by John in Puerto Rico, decided to concentrate on young couples with small children because there was a great need to help this group of people. Having a clear and defined target made it easier to make decisions related to our mission and the style of ministry we would have. During our work, we ministered to other groups of people and we won their confidence (older people, prostitutes, people with AIDS, alcoholics, foreigners) but our specialty and focus was on young couples with children.

Emmanuel, the church Tim pastors, was led in a different direction. While we were convinced God wanted us to focus on the immediate vicinity of our gathering place, we made a conscious decision not to target a specific ethnic or socio-economic subgroup in our diverse community. We pledged to embrace whoever God put in our path. He chose drug addicts and alcoholics as our first step in keeping that promise. It certainly wasn't what we had in mind, but it has borne fruit in a variety of ways. As you get to know your community, God will make it clear who you are to reach.

Identify Stumbling Blocks

The second discovery is the identification of the stumbling blocks the people in your community are likely to face, either on the path to believing or immediately after believing as that fledgling faith is tested. Odds are that there will be 10-20 predictable mini- questions that will need to be addressed on the way to the Big Question of "What will I do with Jesus?" Some will be universal to human nature: Am I ready to admit I am broken and sinful and need God's help? Others will be more culturally specific. For example, in a Christianized society, God's existence may not be a question at all. In a secular community, it may be a big hurdle. In an Islamic community, the shift in the concept of God from a God of hard, unyielding demands to a God of Grace may become the stumbling block. Do I dare break with the traditions and expectations of my family? Is the Bible literature, ancient wisdom, or God's Word? Am I ready to shift from business practices that made me wealthy? What do I do with this new set of sexual boundaries?

The list could be endless, but the idea here is to discover certain themes that rise repeatedly. Perhaps you'll want to map them out like a minefield around the central question of "Am I ready to follow Christ?" Having answers to common questions will help you, and those you train. It will also help with pastoral care and follow-up with those who accept Christ and struggle afterwards with the implications of that decision.

Offer More Than a Sales Pitch

Sometimes evangelism is described as a spiritual sales pitch. The assumption is that the church is trying to sell forgiveness, new life, salvation, or a relationship with Christ the way a used car salesman tries to sell automobiles, but with a better product. The metaphor is limited at best. We do want to present the truth about Christ and we do long to see others embrace him. Indeed, some Christians will approach it in such a way that they will present all the advantages of belonging to Christ while minimizing the costs and will push to "close the deal" that very moment. While we ought not hesitate to ask if someone is ready to make a decision, we do have to recognize that Jesus' model was one that required careful consideration. There were moments when the decision was clear and instantaneous. Jesus indeed called his disciples to come and follow, and they responded immediately. Yet it wasn't the first time they met Jesus. John the Baptist trained and introduced at least two of them first. Coming to faith was a process, and Jesus encouraged those who came to him as volunteers to go back and take some time to count the cost of following so that once they made their choice, they would not turn back.

The point of laying out the map of potential objections is to be prepared to help those you hope to reach count the cost and have a clear picture of the decision they are making. In addition, the map will help you design your ministry in such a way that not just what you say but what you do and how you do it will break down all barriers except the barrier of the gospel itself.

Devise a strategy of witness that encompasses the entire ministry of the church. In a culture that minimizes women or children, it may be valuable to design ministries particularly focused on them. If you hope to reach those in gangs, you will need be used by God to identify ways to establish relationships of trust that will earn the right to be heard, but you will also define strategies that will help them build new lives when they accept Christ. That moment of decision will be preceded and followed by a number of smaller steps that will be essential in getting to that moment and in making it stick. In *Geography of Grace*, Kris Rocke and Joel Van Dyke describe a ministry to gangs that began with a question, "How can we serve you?" The question led to the opening up of some handball courts and then a tournament. Life changing conversations came later. Grace had to be experienced before it could be described, understood and embraced.[32]

Decide How the Whole Church Can Participate

On the occasion when Jesus promised to make the disciples "fishers of men," he didn't hand each one a rod and reel. That wasn't how they fished. They were in boats with at least two men to a boat and they threw out nets and pulled them in as teams. If they got a large catch, other boats with extra fishermen were called in to help haul in the catch. And when Jesus sent them out to visit the villages, he sent them out in pairs. No one went alone. In the same way, it is wise to work together as a congregation. We are always more effective as a team than as a group of individuals. The key is to have a plan for getting as many members as possible involved and training them to play their part.

There are many models for accomplishing this teamwork. Many churches now use small groups as a point of entry. Ideally anyone can invite someone new, but each member in the group adds something to the mix: hospitality, prayer support, explaining Scripture, refreshments, or readiness to serve in other practical ways. Still others try to get as many members involved in targeted ministries to the community with training for identifying opportunities that point back to Christ. One church used a strategy they called Servant Evangelism, in which they went out in groups doing small acts of kindness for strangers: handing out cans of refreshment on a hot day, putting change in parking meters so others could park for free, etc. Most recipients would receive the gift with thanks, but every once in a while, it would spark a conversation that would start a friendship, and eventually, get someone on a path towards Christ. In the meantime, the church members would have fun because they were serving together.

Another approach that has long been popular is an invitation model, where the congregation hosts either a unique event or a designated worship service at a regular interval where the primary responsibility of the members is to invite others so they can hear the gospel explained by someone gifted to do it well.

A third approach involves equipping every member with a simple gospel presentation, often in booklet form, that they are trained to explain themselves, with an invitation to worship as a follow-up step. Evangelism Explosion, Four Spiritual Laws, and Steps to Peace with God are classics. Though they work best in a culture with some Christian understanding, they can be modified to fit a number of different situations.

Tell Our Story and God's Story

One of the most helpful gifts we can offer members of the congregations we serve is the ability to see their own personal stories as they fit in God's story with its themes of Creation, Fall, Redemption, and Restoration. Part of understanding this happens as they come to faith, repenting and believing in Christ. Discipleship fleshes out the larger picture. While salvation is very personal for people, their salvation is only one small piece of God's comprehensive plan.

When members grasp the connection between the two stories—their own story and God's larger plan—they have a natural way to witness in a compelling manner. They simply tell their own story, making connections to the larger story and turning it into an invitation to others to come and join the larger story as well. This transforms a "canned or prepackaged" gospel presentation into a personal, practical account of God's love.

Because the themes in most gospel presentations are rooted in Scripture, any of them could profitably be used to help members draw the connections. But to illustrate, we will use "The Big Story" presentation, adapted from James Choung.[33]

"The Big Story"

The Big Story starts with the world the way it is: messed up. Parts are missing, parts are bent, and parts are broken. Relationships are strained and even disrupted between us as human beings (divorce, crime, competition, jealousy, war), between us and God (feelings of guilt, shame, and lack of purpose or meaning), and us and creation (pollution, global warming, natural disasters). It is fairly easy for us all to agree that this is not life the way it ought to be.

LIFE:
THE WAY IT IS

That very sense that "this is not the way it ought to be" suggests that we innately know that there is a way that it should be. Either it once was something much better or we anticipate that it one day will be much better. Christians believe both to be true. We call the ideal world, the way God made it to be, Creation. We call life the way it is now, the Fall, because by our own selfish desires and greed; we tried to grab control and use it for our benefit, and in the process, we have warped and distorted the world into something less than it could have been.

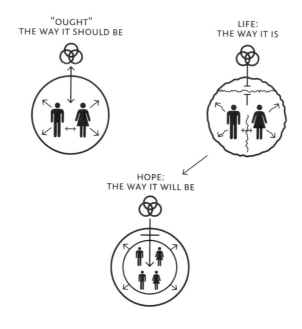

However, we also live in hope that one day this world will be restored. Life will be better. We will experience joy and all the parts of creation will live in harmony again. In fact, you see a great number of organizations out there striving for just that. They are trying to save endangered species, prevent global warming, stop human trafficking, offer marital counseling and job training, etc. There are thousands of ways to improve our world. Yet with all that effort, nothing seems to improve. It's like throwing rocks in the ocean in order to build a bridge between Europe and the Americas—it is simply beyond our capabilities. To see true restoration, we need to turn to the one who created the world in the first place. He is the only one with the resources to do the job, mostly because we have not mastered our own souls or conquered our own selfishness.

The good news is God sent Jesus into our world. Jesus became one of us yet never yielded to selfishness or sin. Instead of grasping for fame, power, or comfort, he sacrificed himself for the rest of us. He invites us to a renewed relationship with God and with each other. He offers forgiveness for the places we have messed up and the power of the Holy Spirit to transform our lives. All we need to do is admit to ourselves and to him how badly we have messed up, invite him to do his work for us and in us, and trust him enough to live life his way instead of our way. That's Redemption.

The reality is that God isn't just redeeming and restoring us as individuals. He is drawing us together as his family, Christ's body, the Church. And he doesn't just leave us sitting on the sidelines as an audience watching while he works. We don't sit on our hands waiting for Christ to return and sort it all out. We have mission, purpose, and meaning. God invites us to join him in what he is doing. We are his agents as he remakes this world.

Helping Others Tell Their Stories

Here are some questions that will help people connect their personal story with the Big Story.

1. How is your life messed up and "fallen?" In what ways is it less than it ought to be?
2. How does that differ from the potential God had for you when he made you? What could have been? What are the circumstances of your life that set you on the path to your personal fall? What are the choices you made that helped bring you down?
3. How did God step into your life? How did you first learn the story of Jesus Christ? How did it move from being a story to a personal conviction that Jesus lived, died, and rose again for you?
4. How has God restored your life? What broken parts have been healed? Which parts are still awaiting healing?
5. What has it meant to you to be a member of God's gathered community? How has he invited you individually and as part of the body to make a difference in this world? How are you an agent of restoration for him?

When people can answer the questions, have them string the answers together into a mini-biography, retelling God's story in their personal stories. If they can't answer one of the questions, it is time to sit down and have a pastoral conversation about the places where they are stuck. Are they having trouble owning the sin in their lives? Is there something about grace they can't comprehend or are refusing to accept? Do they want to stop with salvation instead of accepting God's invitation to be his agents in the world? Or are they trying to fly solo rather than find a place among God's people? The point where they are stuck is a point where God is likely calling them to grow. Help them.

Finally, once members can tell their stories in the context of God's story, ask them to share it with you and with each other before they share it with the world. This accomplishes three things. First, it gets them used to saying the words aloud. Second, it builds confidence as they encourage each other and recognize they are not alone in this. Third, it helps them discern how God works differently in different people's lives within the same framework. That way when they speak with an unbeliever, they have a greater capacity to identify what God is doing in that person's life—the created potential, the sins that will need to be addressed, and most important, how God is beginning to work before the individual even has a clue.

The best part of this approach to training is that members never have to struggle to remember what part comes next or worry about missing an important element. All they need to do is tell their story and what they know already.

The Engel scale below presents steps that can be helpful in identifying where people find themselves in their spiritual pilgrimage. It may be helpful to focus on moving a person along the scale toward a full relationship with Christ.[34]

ENGEL SCALE

+5	Stewardship
+4	Communion with God
+3	Conceptual and behavioural growth
+2	Incorporation into Body
+1	Post-decision evaluation
	New birth
-1	Repentance and faith in Christ
-2	Decision to act
-3	Personal problem recognition
-4	Positive attitude towards gospel
-5	Grasp implications of gospel
-6	Awareness of fundamentals of gospel
-7	Initial awareness of gospel
-8	Awareness of supreme being, no knowledge of gospel

Aubrey Malphurs presents the following principles as key to every evangelistic strategy:

- Go out to find the lost—don't wait for them to come to you!
- Value what God values.
- Understand the perspectives of those you are trying to reach.
- Care for the spiritually needy.
- Adapt methodologies, not the message.
- Seek fertile ground to deposit the seed: find people prepared by the Holy Spirit.
- Clearly communicate the gospel in ways that make sense.
- Fish with many fishing poles: share the gospel with many people in many different ways.
- Accompany evangelism with prayer.
- Seek disciples, not just decisions.
- Work through natural and existing relationships.[35]

A church can ask itself the following questions:

1. What methodology have we used in the past?
2. Which new ones might we try in our changing context?
3. How do we differentiate between "getting decisions" and "discipling" people?

In *The Shaping of Things to Come*, Frost and Hirsch differentiate an incarnational approach from an attractional one for evangelism. The attractional model has a "build it and they will come" attitude. The incarnational approach emphasizes the "sent-ness" of the church and seeks to permeate the culture by going out. It could be freeing to think of evangelism more in terms of a centered set (open system) than a bounded set (closed system).[36] In the bounded set, some people are in and others are out. In the centered set, Christ is at the center. Some people are closer and others are farther, some are in a journey toward him and others are walking away, but all are within the sphere of his reach. It is the Church's call to be witnesses to God's love, forgiveness and acceptance.

BOUNDED SETS VS CENTERED SETS
IN EVANGELISM PERSPECTIVES

BOUNDED
SET

CENTERED
SET

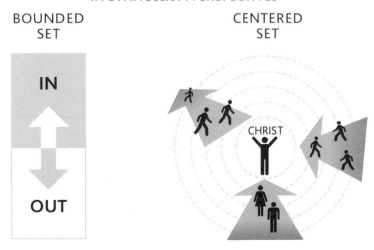

A Damaging Myth

There is a very popular myth that says if a person lives as a good Christian, he or she does not have to say anything to evangelize. This myth assumes people will approach a Christian to find out why he or she is different. This does happen in some cases, but it is dangerous for Christians to rely on their Christian example alone. First of all, many other religions and philosophies have exemplary and admirable followers, but these followers do not have Christ as their Lord. Secondly, relying on testifying only through good works is problematic because a nonbeliever who notices a difference in a Christian's life may then believe people can be saved through their good works. That is exactly the opposite of what we preach. Eternal life is a gift of God, and human beings cannot save themselves. We do good works in gratitude for what God has done first in us (Ephesians 2:8-10). We are saved by grace through faith.

Pursue a Total Encounter with Jesus

There are at least three kind of encounters between a person and Christ. Shaw and Van Engen summarize Kraft's typology of encounters in *Communicating God's Word in a Complex World.*[37]

KRAFT TYPES OF ENCOUNTER

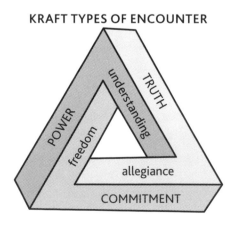

A Power Encounter

This encounter recognizes that God is reconciling the world to himself and that—in Christ—Satan, the enemy, has already been defeated. Through the Spirit of God, the gospel confronts every culture, the power of sin, and the evil one. This reality becomes even more obvious as the second coming of Jesus approaches, when all things will be brought to completion in the new heavens and the new earth. In the meantime, we are in a spiritual battle. The result of a power encounter with Jesus is freedom in Christ. Biblical texts like Ephesians 3:10 and 6:12 make it clear the Church is involved in the struggle against the principalities and powers and not just "against flesh and blood." The battle occurs at cosmic, community, and individual levels. Christ's victory over death, Satan, and evil equips us against the pride still evident in human rebellion and the idolatries of our time (misuse of good things like power, wealth and sex, for example).

Many people in different parts of the world are guided by power. Many respond favorably to the gospel when they understand the changes Christ can make in their lives, their marriages, their families, and their communities. Only Christ fills the emptiness they have and gives them eternal life.

Declaring victory in Christ over the enemy and over sin is a very effective weapon in the church's evangelistic work, but it is incomplete if a balance is not maintained with the other two types of encounters that follow. In the Bible, we see many examples of people who testified to the power of God in their lives but who, nevertheless, did not follow in faith. And in other cases, false teachers also performed miraculous deeds. This should alert us to the fact that an evangelistic strategy based on "power demonstrations" is neither sufficient nor adequate by itself. Sadly, in many churches, this aspect of Christian testimony is being abused to the point that the seriousness of the gospel is ridiculed. Church services sometimes appear like a big show rather than a community of faith.

A Truth Encounter

Here the concept is to know Christ in a true and correct way. This may include academic and theological/philosophical understanding, although it also includes the personal truth of subjective experience. The vehicle for this type of encounter is good teaching. The knowledge of the truth in Jesus Christ allows Christians to interpret and understand the other types of encounters. When the Lord gave a demonstration of his power, he almost always used it to teach his followers. Teaching is what leads a disciple into the truth. It is interesting to note that the favorite title of Jesus for the Holy Spirit is "the Spirit of Truth" (see, for example, John 15-16). What a difference it would make if this biblical truth were recognized!

The Bible also tells us the truth will set us free (see John 8:32). Experiencing the freedom in Christ the Apostle Paul talks about includes not only a power encounter with Jesus, but also an encounter with his truth. The danger here lies in thinking that knowing certain biblical truths and keeping them tenaciously and dogmatically is sufficient for living the Christian life.

A Commitment Encounter

This is the most important of the three encounters. It demands total faithfulness to Jesus Christ and focuses on the person's submission to the lordship of Jesus. This involves a lifelong journey of obedience and service to God. Believers submit their will to the Lord through his Word, and after recognizing the power of God and being taught in his ways, they submit their lives to God through a serious and faithful commitment. This is the command of discipleship.

Ultimately, this is an encounter of love. The testimony of the Christian and that of the community of faith must include all three types of encounters. As Michael Green points out in *The Local Church: Agent of Evangelization*, we need loving, vibrant local churches to demonstrate the Christian faith in word and deed, thoughtfully and consistently, to their communities.[38]

Foster Love and Unity, the Foundations of Evangelism

Love and unity in the church are vital in maintaining an effective evangelistic program. It doesn't matter what strategy your church develops if there isn't unity and love in the community where the newly converted person will be nourished. Love and unity give strength and an authentic testimony to the congregation. In John 13:34-35, we read that others will recognize we are disciples of Christ by the love we show amongst ourselves. If these elements do not exist, we will not be able to retain the fruit won through evangelism. Growth in a united and loving congregation is not automatic; there are loving congregations that decline for other reasons. But the absence of these characteristics will make evangelistic efforts much more difficult. John 17 repeats the part of Jesus' prayer that asks that we should be one as Christ and the Father are one, and Jesus adds, "to let the world know that you sent me." Witness is connected to unity.

Preach the Gospel

Another part of the evangelistic function is preaching the gospel. What follows are some guidelines from an experienced preacher.

We include this section for many young church planters in the Multiplication Network training. Feel free to skip to the next chapter.

CONSTRUCTING THE SERMON

The sermon. By following the advice we are including here, even pastors whose gifts are not particularly strong in public preaching can become faithful communicators of the Word. For most people who have recently come to know Jesus, their expectation when hearing a sermon is clear: they want to learn about God and how to make him real in their daily life.

The audience and their world. To effectively connect with our audience, we need to be aware of what is happening in their world. Preachers are notorious for ignoring literature and the arts, as well as the meaning of newsworthy events in the global framework of our time. We should be sensitive to the spiritual needs of the congregation. And since the majority of the church planter's congregation consists of new converts, we should keep the level of our preaching at the level of their biblical knowledge and spiritual growth.

Good preaching will combine the two worlds. A review I usually use to assure myself I have addressed all the important areas when preparing to preach is the following:

Message (content): The message I have comes from the Word of God. Its content is biblical, relevant, and interesting.
Conviction (authority): I am convinced of what I am preaching. The message is profoundly rooted in my heart.
Passion (urgency): I am concerned for the hearers. I love them and I know what's going on when I bring them the Word of God. My heart should reflect God's desires and intention as revealed through his Word.
Anointing (divine backing): God backs up his Word and his messenger. Only God can give this.

The first of these four elements is related to the interaction of the preacher and his audience with the Word. The next two have to do with the effect of the Word on the preacher himself or herself. The last element has to do with God and his relationship with the preacher in the exercise of preaching.

Here are three vital elements for preparing a good sermon. Remember, however, that preaching should not be a mechanical science but rather a spiritual art.

1.   **Concentrate on one idea.** The temptation to preach "all the wisdom of God" in just one sermon is common in those who are beginning in the privilege of preaching. Once the text has been studied conscientiously, we should center ourselves on its principal idea and make that the axis of the sermon. It is better to present one biblical idea solidly than to speak on many themes superficially. "One sermon, one idea" is one of the best pieces of advice I received as a young preacher. The central idea should come from the biblical text. Sometimes we do not see it due to the following obstacles:

A preconceived idea. We see in the text what we want it to say.

A borrowed idea. We see what another (a preacher or biblical commentator) says the text says.

A peripheral idea. We see something the text says, but it is not what is most important.

A preferred idea. We always see the same thing, no matter what text we are using. Someone has wisely said that if, out of all the tools, we are familiar only with the hammer, then all the problems we see will look like nails.

2. **Build a solid argument.** Clarity and strength in developing the argument will contribute enormously to the understanding of the principal idea and the impetus for hearers to apply it to their lives. In talking about argument, we are referring to the development of our principal point, so that its biblical basis, relevance for the hearer, and spiritual implications can be appreciated. A good argument persuades its hearers to obedience.

3. **Build an understandable outline.** The importance of an outline is obvious. It helps the preacher as well as the hearer. It helps the preacher to maintain order in the development of ideas, to stay on topic, to line up the points in order, to remember the elements, and to maintain the unity of the sermon. The outline helps the hearer to follow the logic of the argument and its progression, as well as to remember its content.

The outline should have at least three parts:

The introduction. The introduction will determine the attitude and the attention of the hearers. A good introduction presents the topic and shows its relevance; it raises people's interest and provokes curiosity. It should be brief, entertaining, and interesting. It is my practice to write the introduction and to memorize it. This helps me to overcome the initial impact of nervousness and to be sure of a good beginning to the sermon.

The body. The body is the content, the "meat" of the sermon. It should move logically toward and around the central idea. In good expository preaching, the subdivisions of the body, or the "points of the sermon" as they are often called, will come from the actual biblical text.

The conclusion. Like the introduction, the conclusion has a disproportionate importance compared with its length. It is the last opportunity to assure ourselves that we have clearly transmitted our central idea. Many times the last thing that is heard is remembered the best. The conclusion can be a summary, a question that moves people to application, or an illustration that impacts the heart. The most common error is to draw out the conclusion indefinitely, like an airplane that seems like it is going to land but never does. I learned from my mentor that I should not "try to do what the

Holy Spirit has not done yet." Other common errors are preaching another sermon, digressing until the audience sleeps, introducing new outside ideas to the sermon, and forcing the theme of the cross of Jesus.

ILLUSTRATIONS

Illustrations are important because they help to clarify and explain, to demonstrate a possible application in real life, to convince people of sin (as the prophet Nathan did with King David), to lower people's resistance though the use of humor, to inspire and motivate to action (as Jesus and the parable of the Good Samaritan), to make the truth memorable ("passing a camel through the eye of a needle"), to increase interest in the sermon, and to help to record a concept in the minds of the hearers. They may be taken from the Bible, daily life, our reading, the news, or even a book of illustrations. However, the best illustrations are the ones that come from our own experiences.

When we use illustrations, we must be careful that they do not become the reason for the sermon or its center. If we are not careful, illustrations can be a distraction in the sermon or an act of sabotage that destroys the sermon—when we tell a story that is out of place, when we use humor inadequately, or when we give an illustration that is "stronger" (or better) than the sermon.

TO FINISH

The world needs to hear God. It is a privilege for us to preach. God is on our side in our humble efforts at speaking in his name. His Spirit intends to use us. In our weakness we can, as did the Apostle Paul, allow the power of God to show itself and through us the eternal message of God can be heard by a world that needs it so much—and we, blessing of blessings, will have been the vehicle.

Soli Deo Gloria.
Rev. José Martinez[39]

"The Great Commission is not an option to be considered.
It is an order to be obeyed."
-Hudson Taylor (1832-1905)[40]*-*
[Missionary to China]

COMPELLING WITNESS

Survey Questions

Mark the following survey on a scale of 1-10, 1 being a total disagreement, and 10 a total agreement. After finishing your evaluation of all seven phrases, add it up and divide by seven to get a general average for this vital sign. Then consider the questions below.

1. Our church has a clear plan to reach the community with the Good News of the Kingdom.	
2. Our church is active in building relationships with the unbelievers of our community.	
3. Our church trains and equips its members to give witness in the community.	
4. I've been personally trained to contribute to the evangelistic efforts of the church.	
5. I feel personally involved in the evangelistic task of our congregation.	
6. I can identify new people in our church who came in the past year as a result of my evangelistic efforts.	
7. Our church participates in world mission efforts.	

AVERAGE

For Discussion

1. What observations do you have regarding the results of the survey?

2. Which question made you think the most? Why?

3. What one simple step can you take to strengthen this vital sign?

Second Function
COMPREHENSIVE DISCIPLESHIP

The Church helps people to see Jesus clearly and to know his will for their lives. It equips them to follow him in all aspects of life.

"They devoted themselves to the apostles' teaching..."
(Acts 2:42)

The early church understood clearly that its foundation was the teaching of Jesus. The word "doctrine" means teaching. The disciples studied the teachings of the apostles, repeatedly reviewed them, and practiced them. They used the framework of those teachings to evaluate every new idea. Even the Jews of the synagogue in Berea analyzed what Paul had told them according to the Scriptures (Acts 17:11). The passage continues: "Many of them believed!"

"Disciple" (mathetes in Greek) means one who learns, but more akin to apprentice than student. The disciple follows Jesus and learns from him, but not just head knowledge. Discipleship requires absorbing behavior, character, attitudes, perspectives—a total worldview. When Jesus gave the Great Commission in Matthew 28, he commanded the apostles not only to baptize but also to teach to fully follow Christ's teachings. They were not to simply dispense doctrine but also instruction in how to live out truths from God's Word. Being a disciple, therefore, requires one to persevere in both the study of God's Word and the incorporation of those truths into one's life. This was the foundation of the early church. And it should be the foundation today for every congregation that is serious and committed to the Lord.

In Ephesians 4, Paul calls us to Christian maturity. The gospels say that we should be like children in terms of our faith, but this does not mean that we are to be childish or immature. Paul says we should no longer be "infants, tossed back and forth by the waves," but rather we should grow up into Christ, who is the Head (Ephesians 4:14-15). The author of Hebrews tells some Christians:

> In fact, though by this time you ought to be teachers, you need someone to teach you the elementary truths of God's word all over again. You need milk, not solid food! Anyone who lives on milk, being still an infant, is not acquainted with the teaching about righteousness. But solid food is for the mature...(Hebrews 5:12-14a)

Healthy church ministry should include a special emphasis on discipleship toward Christian maturity. Every church needs a solid foundation in the knowledge of Jesus and a commitment to his message. Without followers of Jesus Christ, there can be neither worship, nor fellowship in Christ, nor evangelism, nor Christian service. A church that practices holistic growth will pay a lot of attention to this function of its calling and will practice what 2 Peter 3:18 says: "But grow in the grace and knowledge of our Lord and Savior Jesus Christ." In practical terms, this means that as part of its ministry, a healthy church provides a number of opportunities for people to grow spiritually in discipleship. The church's weekly and monthly calendars should show that there are many possibilities for learning and personal growth.

There is a debate among some theologians whether or not evangelism and discipleship should be separated. The first has the second as its objective. The distinction is much the same as that between prenatal and postnatal care of infants. One is in preparation of birth. The other grows from birth to maturity. The initial moment when we believe opens the way to the process of discipleship.

At the same time, it is important to note the vital connection between evangelism and discipleship. They flow from one directly to the other. The process is largely the same in both. Both work incarnationally as both unbelievers and growing believers see and experience the teachings of Christ animated in the lives of believers. Both are communal, becoming richer and more fully balanced as the body of believers each invest their strengths and insights into the mix. Both happen in stages, often messy stages, as we relinquish parts of our lives to Christ while continuing to retain, often subconsciously, other portions. While our salvation may be secure in Christ, even mature believers continue to require a fresh application of the gospel as the Spirit continues his saving work.

Still the foundation of our "new birth" marks a fundamental turning point that makes the distinction between evangelism and discipleship helpful. For the purpose of this study, we regard evangelism as the responsibility to communicate the gospel to every human being and to search out the lost. In this section, we will analyze discipleship as the process of sanctification in which we surrender ourselves more each day in obedience and faithfulness to God and join in His mission.

"Persons who learn"

As we saw previously, mathetes means one who learns. The word "mathematics" is derived from this word. We may not like to learn mathematics, but those who say they are Christians must learn to follow the Lord. We are apprentices and followers of the Lord. Luke 6:25-35, perhaps one of the most demanding passages about discipleship, orders us to renounce everything in order to be Christ's disciples. Jesus says, "Anyone who does not carry his cross and follow me cannot be my disciple" (Luke 14:27). Discipleship, therefore, has to do with a total surrender to the Lord Jesus Christ, a surrender that includes all aspects of the relationship between the believer and God.

DIMENSIONS OF DISCIPLESHIP

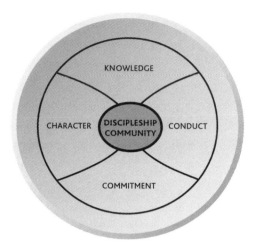

It is a mistake to think discipleship is a set of programs to teach the Bible. In reality, discipleship has several dimensions that help to promote spiritual maturity. To remember the central aspects of the process of spiritual maturity, it can be helpful to recognize that discipleship consists of knowing, doing, being, and willing; also, it promotes growth using head, hands, and heart. These are simple ways of expressing that there cannot be spiritual growth if one is not growing in knowledge, conduct, character, and commitment.

Knowledge: Knowing

Biblical knowledge always develops on two different levels. One is focused on the content. There are a variety of Biblical concepts we need to comprehend and tuck away in our brains: that there is a God, that he made us and the world we are in, that the human race corrupted his creation including ourselves by our sin, and that he sent his Son into this world to set things right. The list goes on:

the Trinity, the Holy Spirit, providence, grace, resurrection, and so on. Long term it is difficult to grow in faith without growing in an understanding of the content of that faith.

However, as James points out, even the demons know God exists (James 2:19), but it doesn't do them much good. Scriptural knowledge isn't just content. It is relational. It means having the assurance that all of those Bible facts have application to one's personal life. I am fearfully and wonderfully made. I am redeemed and forgiven. Jesus is my Savior and Lord. The Father has adopted me and the Spirit has filled me. Part of the task of discipleship is coming to the realization that all of those wonderful biblical doctrines are true for me personally. That is the type of knowledge that becomes transformative in every area of life, hands and heart as well as head.

Conduct: Doing

Conduct is one of the most evident ways to show the fruit of what God is doing in our lives. We should create good habits that shape our lives, such as dedicating time to prayer, to Bible study, and to family recreation. Sometimes we replace obedience with merely the knowledge of biblical teachings. James instructs us: "Do not merely listen to the word, and so deceive yourselves. Do what it says" (1:22). Our conduct should complement our biblical knowledge. The way we conduct ourselves in the Christian life will be one of the methods that God will use to make his gospel known. We are, in a way, the open Bible before the nonbelieving community.

Often times, it is assumed that knowledge is the leading edge of discipleship, that knowledge will shape our behavior. However, the opposite is also often true. Only when we act on our faith do we get a true understanding of what God would teach us. A prime example is Abraham, who really only begins to know God after he leaves his homeland for an unknown destination to which God would lead him. Just as one doesn't become a carpenter by pounding nails, one doesn't become a disciple without turning the other cheek and forgiving others as we have been forgiven, for example. This, of course, does not excuse us from the responsibility of studying and examining the Scriptures. Knowledge complements conduct.

Character: Being

This aspect of our personhood is being forged blow by blow on the anvil of life and in the context of community. Character is often described as who we are when no one else is looking. The Christian's character grows in maturity in the measure that the person submits all of his or her life to the Lordship of Jesus Christ. The person sees things with the eyes of Christ and develops a perspective on life and the world—a worldview—more in tune with that of God and his Word. Character goes much deeper than an isolated action that we perform. It is something that we work on long-term. This old proverb sums it up well: "It takes a second to make a hero, but it takes an entire life to make a good man."

Commitment: Willing

When we submit our will to Christ, we turn everything over to him. In this endeavor, commitment is necessary because we often balk at following Christ. What he asks of us may not make sense to us, may require sacrifice, or may be contrary to our own desires and plans. In such moments, it requires a Spirit-aided act of the will to steel ourselves to do what we know is right. Jesus evidenced that kind of determination as he came down from the glorious experience of the Transfiguration in Luke 19. In that moment, Luke tells us, Jesus "set his face" to go to Jerusalem and face the cross. The early Christians also inspire us: with their blood they planted the seed of the gospel. In a time like the one in which we live, it is even more important to take note of the commitment that arises from a real transformation in Jesus Christ. It is God himself who is perfecting us and strengthening us through committed discipleship. Let's listen to what the Word of God tells us:

> Be self-controlled and alert. Your enemy the devil prowls around like a roaring lion looking for someone to devour. Resist him, standing firm in the faith, because you know that your brothers throughout the world are undergoing the same kind of sufferings. And the God of all grace, who called you to his eternal glory in Christ, after you have suffered a little while, will himself restore you and make you strong, firm, and steadfast (1 Peter 5:8-10).

A Profound Transformation

Discipleship also depends on a change of worldview—a new way to see and interpret the world and reality. A biblical worldview covers all areas of life and does not allow the segmentation of faith. The following diagrams show the difference between a segmented and an integrated view of faith and life.

A SEGMENTED VIEW VS. AN INTEGRATED VIEW OF FAITH AND LIFE

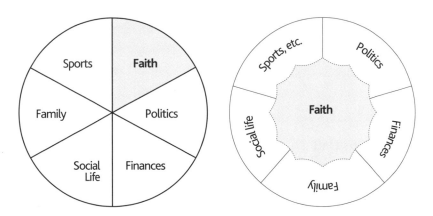

Faith should affect and influence every sphere of life. A biblical worldview should affect the values that drive our actions, our behaviors, and our attitudes. These in turn will have consequences that should glorify God. The consequences of a biblical worldview are generally good and positive. For example, an alcoholic changes his way of thinking and seeing life and now treats his wife better, teaches his children, and takes care of his finances. But sometimes the consequences of having a biblical worldview can bring suffering or persecution, as in the case of a person who converts to Christianity in a Muslim context and is then rejected by the rest of the community. In any case, the goal of discipleship is to bring about a radical change in a person's worldview, leading to the transformation of the rest of his or her life.

BIBLICAL WORLDVIEW AS FOUNDATION FOR DISCIPLESHIP

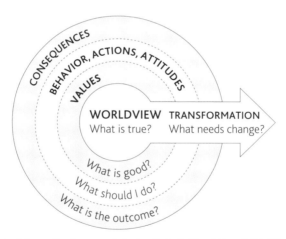

Adapted from *Sembremos Iglesias Saludables*, Miami: Unilit, p. 275.

Learning by Doing

Discipleship needs to be both a combination of formation and practice. If everything the local church does is practice (activity), without time for reflection, it will not produce the desired result. In the same way, pure "class" time (passivity), without any practice or action, will also fail to produce fruit. According to Hesselgrave, learning in discipleship can include formal (in a class), informal (imitated and modeled), or technical (practicing one's abilities) dimensions.[41] A model that uses cycles of study and practice is very useful for developing leaders and disciples in the local church. We recommend that each church leader try to come up with a study series, combined with ministry, to help the disciples take the next step in their growth in the faith. Some church planters teach the steps to maturity described in 2 Peter 1:5-7: faith, then goodness, knowledge, self-control, etc. Others use a chronological system to teach the Scriptures, choose topics according to situations that arise in the church and the community, or follow outlines and patterns previously developed by their denomination.

Putting It All Together

Developing a comprehensive, congregational approach to discipleship that effectively mixes all of the ingredients listed above is as complex and varied as the people it hopes to cultivate. However, the task becomes more manageable when visualized in terms of tools and outcomes.

Tools

Discipleship tools fall into two basic categories: Information and Practice. Think of it in terms of learning a musical instrument. There is an element of knowledge. There are notes and chords, scales and rhythms that need to be firmly planted in one's head. Still they are not mastered until they are practiced frequently enough that one's fingers can play them smoothly without deliberate thought.

So too discipleship starts with content. Followers of Christ need to have a grasp of Scripture, particularly the story of Christ himself. His birth, his character, his teaching, his miracles, his love, and his anger, his death and his resurrection--all are lessons to be absorbed. The basics of Christian doctrine are also essential lessons used to understand the Christian faith. So the first question to be answered will be, which stories should be taught first? And the second, how will they be taught? The best setting is not always a classroom. Some of these lessons may be incorporated into sermons, devotionals, and personal reflections. Other lessons will be brought to bear when one discusses how to tackle a particular problem in the disciple's or church's life.

This leads to the second tool of discipleship: practice. The disciple can engage in activities that develop the "muscle memory" of Christian habits. Disciples can pray together in worship, in small groups, in family settings, as well as one-on-one. This way they can learn the feel and rhythm of prayer. They can tackle a portion of Scripture together devotionally so they have a sense of what personal time in God's Word can feel like. Christian service, working side-by-side with someone, is also a key ingredient in the formation of a disciple. Reflecting afterwards, noting not only results but attitudes, can also be helpful. Engaging in Christian fellowship in small groups and with the congregation as a whole also nurtures the habits of the heart.

Let the content of the tenets of faith and the practice of faith cross-pollinate into a variety of methods of spiritual formation. In that way you will have an ever growing box of discipleship tools which each blend content and practice to uniquely fit the situation. After a while, each leader and each congregation will find their favorite tools that become as familiar as hammer and screwdriver to a builder.

Outcomes

While information and practice are both vital to discipleship, the goal is never to pass a Bible test or to be an expert in spiritual disciplines. A comprehensive discipleship process will seek two outcomes.

The first is Christ-shaped lives. As Paul puts it in Ephesians 4:23-24, "[You were taught] to be made new in the attitude of your minds; and to put on the new self, created to be like God in true righteousness and holiness." Our measure is not whether we know the right things or do the right things but whether we reflect the character of Christ. After one year or five, will the people we disciple exhibit more of the fruits of the Spirit: love, joy, peace, forbearance, kindness, goodness, faithfulness, gentleness, and self-control (Galatians 5:22-23)? Will their spouses, children, friends, and co-workers endorse a positive change? Over and over the New Testament indicates that true discipleship will be reflected in how we treat others, from our brothers and sisters in Christ (1 John) to those with a different ethnic and religious background (parable of the Good Samaritan). Jesus' ultimate litmus test is how we treat the most vulnerable and powerless when no one else is looking (Matthew 25:31-46). Discipleship is rooted in the teaching of scripture and the formation of Christian habits, but it finds its home in our hearts and relationships.

Yet there is a second outcome that discipleship aims for as well: Passing it on. Gospel-centered formation will lead to multiplication. When we integrate Christ into our lives or ours into Christ, the natural result is a desire to let others in on our discovery, to share our story, to share HIS story. There is no room for spiritual gluttony where we keep absorbing more and more of Christ's blessings without spilling that life over into others. For some, this expression is direct and verbal as they share their faith evangelistically. Others show their gratitude forward by discipling others. Paul teaches his disciple, Timothy: "And the things you have heard me say in the presence of many witnesses entrust to reliable men who will also be qualified to teach others" (2 Timothy 2:2).

PAUL   TIMOTHY   FAITHFUL MEN   OTHERS

2 TIMOTHY 2:2

Evangelism and discipleship are particularly verbal expressions of Christ's work in our lives. However, non-verbal displays of devotion are equally important. These can range from the arts as in the case of Bezalel, the artisan in charge of the construction of the Tabernacle in Exodus 35, to ministries of compassion such as Dorcas in Acts 9 to generosity (2 Corinthians 9:11-12) to simple hospitality as with the widows in 1 Timothy 5. The ways in which the impact of grace is displayed vary from disciple to disciple according to the spiritual gifts they have been given. This is why helping members explore their gifts is a vital part of the discipleship process. It equips them to pass on what they have received in such a way that anyone they meet will take note.

For a model of what discipleship should look like, study the Gospels, watching particularly how Jesus dealt with his own disciples. The best summary comes from the Apostle Paul who touches on the content (the message of Christ) and the practices (teaching, admonishing, singing) to end result of Christ-shaped character (gratitude in your hearts) passed on to others in word and deed in the name of Jesus.

Let the message of Christ dwell among you richly as you teach and admonish one another with all wisdom through psalms, hymns, and songs from the Spirit, singing to God with gratitude in your hearts. And whatever you do, whether in word or deed, do it all in the name of the Lord Jesus, giving thanks to God the Father through him. (Ephesians 3:16-17)

FOR DISCUSSION

The graphic below shows a discipleship model which should be one integrated whole, combining discipling strategies for the Body and community. It is shown in two diamonds for conversation purposes, but should be appreciated with a "both/ and" approach. According to the authors, the Christian life is incomplete playing only on one diamond. What do you think of this statement?

DISCIPLESHIP DIAMOND

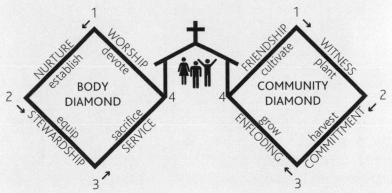

Adapted from *Creating Communities of the Kingdom*, Shenk & Stutzman, 1988, p159.

"Those who teach doctrine must first teach by their lives, else they pull down with one hand what they build up with the other."
-Matthew Henry, 1662-1714[42]-

COMPREHENSIVE DISCIPLESHIP

Survey Questions

Mark the following survey on a scale of 1-10, 1 being a total disagreement, and 10 a total agreement. After finishing your evaluation of all seven phrases, add it up and divide by seven to get a general average for this vital sign. Then consider the questions below.

1. The church promotes practices of education and discipleship appropriate to all ages.	
2. Our teachers are effective in discipling/teaching our members.	
3. When a new person accepts Christ, he or she is immediately discipled by someone.	
4. As time goes on, it becomes increasingly evident that the members live under the guidance of the Spirit.	
5. The church is helping me grow spiritually.	
6. I am a member of a small group that helps me grow spiritually.	
7. Our church promotes a life of prayer.	

AVERAGE

For Discussion

1. What observations do you have regarding the results of the survey?

2. Which question made you think the most? Why?

3. What one simple step can you take to strengthen this vital sign?

Third Function
COMPASSIONATE SERVICE

*The Church meets people's needs in the name of Christ
and invites them to be disciples.*

"Selling their possessions and goods, they gave to
anyone as he had need" (Acts 2:45).

The early church shared its goods among the faithful and also gave to people in need. This impressed the people living around the church and testified to the strength of Christian love. The internal change Christ had made in their lives showed in external works that changed society. Spiritual transformation carried with it a social and community commitment. Although we know from other texts that not everyone sold their property, many did so to help the common good. This is very much in agreement with what we read in the book of James, when he says that "faith without works is dead" (2:17). Works demonstrate one's transformation by grace in Jesus Christ. And although works do not contribute to salvation which is by grace alone (Ephesians 2:8-9), they help us to live the Christian life in a dynamic and edifying way. In theological terms, works do not fall under justification, but under the sanctification of the believer. Sanctification—holiness—involves being *set apart*. Unfortunately, a large part of the church has only focused on being *set apart FROM* and has neglected the other dimension of being *set apart FOR*. In other words, a true vocation of holiness is not just a separateness "from the patterns of this world" (Romans 12:2) but a call into mission and service in the world, joining the Spirit in his transformative activity in the world.

MODELS OF CHURCH IN RELATIONSHIP TO THE WORLD

ENGAGE
Emphasizes cultural engagement.
Holiness means participating in God's
redemptive reign and restoration of all
things in Christ as salt and light.

ESCAPE
Emphasizes separateness from the world.
Holiness means "stay clean."

ACCOMODATE
Emphasizes identification with the world
to the extent that the gospel is compromised.
Holiness is exchanged for cultural conformity.

The graphic above helps explain there are churches whose self-understanding is to be separate from the world. These churches usually emphasize the "other-world" aspects of the gospel. On the other extreme are churches who want to identify with the surrounding culture so much that they compromise the integrity of the gospel. A healthy church will have a balanced and contextual approach to incarnating the values of the gospel and engage culture with the claims of Christ. There is a wide range of callings for the church that span from evangelism to working for justice and creation care.

A healthy church will be able to identify its own tradition (such as Contemplative, Holiness movement, Charismatic, Pentecostal, Evangelical, Incarnational, etc.) and yet find its contribution to the Church and to the world.

Considerations of this vital sign of a healthy church must be framed in terms of creation theology. Serving the world is part of the cultural mandate to the people of God to steward all of creation for God's glory. Serving others in a fallen world, led by the Spirit, is a way of participating with God in bringing about redemption and recreation within the world. The biblical narrative bookends the role of God's people as participation in God's mission to bring back all things into right relationship with God (fixing the mess of the Garden) but, more than that, looking forward in hope to the beautiful, ordered society in the new city where all things will be as they should be.

Bringing all things to right relationship with God involves unmasking the principalities and powers which were disarmed in Christ's death and resurrection. The Holy Spirit empowers the Church to do this work in all kinds of ways. Ephesians 4 tells us that each member of the body is gifted for a particular kind of activity of service and testimony. The entire body, working together, is involved in helping to build one another up and in sharing with those who are in need. Ephesians 2:10 tells us, "We are God's workmanship, created in Christ Jesus to do good works, which God prepared in advance for us to do." The command to serve is clear. Jesus himself said that he did not come to be served, but to serve (Matthew 20:28).

In the previous section on Text and Context, we highlighted the power of compassionate service in the early church. Their willingness to risk their own lives in service to others during a series of plagues gave early believers credibility. Their bravery earned respect and a receptive ear, particularly among those they nursed back to health. At the same time, these early Christians embraced the marginalized of their society. Those who were slaves were welcomed as brothers and sisters in Christ at the same communion table as the slave owners. Some indeed were set free (cf. Paul's letter to Philemon). Women were also granted a higher place than in most corners of society. In pagan culture, female infants were often abandoned, but Christians refused to abandon children and even started orphanages to care for them. Widows without children were also taken in and cared for by the community.

The Old Testament, in particular, emphasizes the need for God's people to exhibit justice. This was codified in the laws on gleaning, slavery, inheritance, lending, and the year of Jubilee to make sure that the most vulnerable in society were protected. Later, when these laws were ignored, the prophets offered up that lack of justice as one of God's primary complaints against his people, focusing especially on a quartet of the powerless: widows, orphans, foreigners, and the poor. This history as well as Jesus' example and teaching shaped the early church.

Without Service, It's Worthless

The church that worships and maintains good communion among the flock but does not serve others is incomplete. All Christians should find their place of service to God by finding ministries that use their God-given gifts. Whether it's something simple, like sweeping a meeting place, or very complex, like fighting against oppression and injustice, each Christian must participate in an area of service individually and corporately. This function of the church cannot be missing in a congregation that wishes to grow in a holistic and healthy way. It is the responsibility of the leadership to help place each member in a role of service and ministry for the edification of the Body of Christ and the glory of God.

The good thing about the definition above is that although it is brief, it includes a holistic witness to the nonbelieving world. Howard Snyder, in *Perspectives on the World Christian Movement*, says that the church is much more than God's tool for evangelism and social change; it is God's instrument for carrying out his entire cosmic plan.[43] A biblical worldview integrates all aspects of life under the lordship of Jesus, and there is not a sphere that is outside his dominion and interest in redemption. All the institutions that God has created belong to him, and they exist to fulfill his purposes of transformation.

"There is not a square inch in the whole domain of our human existence over which Christ, who is Sovereign over all, does not cry: 'Mine!'"
-Abraham Kuyper, Pastor and Prime Minister of Holland, 1901- 1905[44]

The Church cannot have a compelling witness without compassionate service. The church should avoid falling into reductionism. The serious Christian should not divorce actions from words. It all goes together, in one package, although sometimes one aspect is emphasized more than another depending on the circumstances. For example, at the end of the last century, Hurricane Georges passed through the Caribbean, devastating much of Puerto Rico, the Dominican Republic, Haiti, and Cuba. Not even two months later, Hurricane Mitch slammed Honduras and Nicaragua in Central America. Many churches and Christian organizations from all over the world answered the call to help Christians and non-Christians in those countries. The amount of help was impressive and motivating. House construction, medical assistance, food, and clothing for those whose homes were destroyed, and the huge number of volunteers who helped in the situation, preached more than the best sermon could.

For this reason, we need a holistic strategy that understands evangelism and social activism as the two parts of a pair of scissors or the two wings of a bird. With just one side, scissors do not cut; with one wing, a bird doesn't fly. What happens if we row on just one side of a boat? The boat will just go in circles. It won't move forward. Likewise, we cannot present a compelling testimony to the world if we do not integrate social action with evangelism.

We need a holistic strategy that understands both the importance of evangelization as well as the importance of social action. It is all part of a single witness in Jesus Christ. When we integrate good works with evangelism, we can make a big impact in the community. Social action can open a way for verbal proclamation but must not be the sole motivation for it. The danger here is simply using our service as bait to accomplish our hidden agenda. When we cease to serve out of a primary purpose of love, it not only ceases to be authentic service, it also ceases to be compelling witness because the compassion of Christ that makes it compelling will be absent. It is vital that we serve with no strings attached, leaving the results to the Holy Spirit. When we serve out of a heart of gratitude for what we have received from Christ and a heart of love for those we serve, the Holy Spirit will use our efforts, but at his discretion: sometimes to reach those we serve, sometimes to grow us, and often both at the same time.

There have always been big debates between churches and denominations due to the tension that exists when trying to find a balance between social action (sometimes in socio-political forms) and evangelism. Although it is rare to find Christians who only believe in one extreme of this polarity and who completely reject the other absolutely, we can make some observations about each end of the continuum. Those who emphasize social action, in general, emphasize the kingdom in its visible, earthly expression. These people work to establish the reign of God here and now. Often this approach is called the "Social Gospel," and its promoters are sometimes accused of trying to build a utopian society. They see Jesus as an agent of change or even as a revolutionary. They fight for justice and peace. They emphasize institutional and systemic sin in social structures rather than moral sin of people as individuals. They fight against poverty, racism, oppression, and unemployment. This type of testimony tries to attract people through the good works of the Christian community. Social action and political intervention are the key tools, and the incarnation of Jesus is one of its theological anchors.

On the other pole, the side of evangelism, people emphasize the salvation of souls for the kingdom of heaven. They are frequently accused of worrying more about the future situation of the soul than for the actual situation of the human being. Some say that they are not worried about the body or about social realities "because all that is passing away." They see Jesus as the savior of souls. These people would say that in order to change society, we need to transform people one heart at a time. When a person is converted to Jesus Christ and repents of his or her sins, then society is transformed. Verbal proclamation and preaching are the key tools of this side and Christ's work on the cross is its main theological anchor.

The evangelical world, with representatives from many countries, came together to discuss this issue in the International Consultation on the Relationship between Evangelism and Social Responsibility, held in Grand Rapids, Michigan (USA), in 1982. This meeting was sponsored by the Lausanne Committee for World Evangelization and the World Evangelical Fellowship.[45] During this event, the representatives agreed that the divorce between evangelism and social responsibility reflected a dualistic thinking, dividing the spiritual and the physical. While the Bible distinguishes between the two, it teaches that they are related and should be kept together.

At the conference, the relationship between evangelism and social responsibility was discussed in depth, and the participants recognized that social action can have three types of healthy relationships with evangelism:

(1) Social action as a **CONSEQUENCE** of evangelism. God changes people when they are born again, and their new life is made evident in the way that they serve others. In 1 John 3:16-18, the Scripture teaches us to show the love that God gave us by loving our brothers and sisters, serving their needs, and being ready to give our own lives for them. In *Generous Justice*, Tim Keller points out that the terms *justification and justice* both have the same root.[46] They are intimately tied together. That fact that we have been justified by Christ out of his deep love for us when we did not deserve it compels us to seek justice for those most vulnerable, even if they don't deserve it. We are compelled to reflect our Savior.

(2) Social action as a **BRIDGE** to evangelism. Many times Jesus healed or acted with mercy toward people before proclaiming to them the good news. Social action for our neighbors causes them to pay more attention when we speak to them about the gospel but is good in and of itself. Helping nonbelievers when they are going through material problems allows us to get to the more profound needs of eternal salvation. As an African proverb says, "Empty stomachs do not have ears." Social action opens doors and ears, and it builds bridges to those who haven't heard the gospel.

(3) Social action as a **COMPANION** to evangelism. In the letter of James, we see that faith and works go together. We know that we do good works in gratitude for the faith that God gives us, and that they facilitate a living and productive faith that benefits others. In the same way *diakonía* (ministry of service and mercy) and *kerygma* (proclamation of the gospel) are united.

Transforming salvation not only includes people who are forgiven of their particular sins, but it also seeks to change unjust structures that promote systemic and institutional sin (like racism, economic oppression, unethical legal systems, etc.). Look for the way that your church can participate in service to your community according to its needs, and you will see the Lord transforming lives and communities with a holistic gospel.

New Heaven and New Earth

The healthy church is participating in God's grand project of redeeming and restoring all aspects of life in and through Christ. The problem of sin has brought distortion and brokenness to the relationships of each person with God, self, others, and creation. Part of the church's role in society is to help make these lines less blurry. Passages like Colossians 1 and 2 Corinthians 5 teach us that we are "reconcilers" and "ambassadors." The Church helps bring healing and justice and right relationship between the different aspects of God's creation.

The following graphic helps explain this truth.

HEALTHY VS. DISTORTED RELATIONSHIPS

Adapted from Bryant L. Myers, *Walking with the Poor: Principles and Practices of Transformational Development* (Maryknoll, N.Y.: Orbis Books 1999), 27.

Isaiah 65 and Revelation 21 teach us that God is bringing about a new heaven and a new earth. This is the end game: the renewal and restoration of all things in Christ. While only God can make this happen, he invites the Church to participate with him in this recreation activity and to be a foretaste of the kingdom that Jesus inaugurated with his coming to Earth. The Church acts as a demonstration plot for the wider world.

Therefore, while service can have a very practical expression in the diaconal function of the church, we must also hold a more ample perspective of the whole church as a servant in the world that brings hope as the expression of the Servant King who is restoring all things unto himself. Healthy churches, then, not only serve others but have an open invitation to all to join the community of the Spirit that is recreating, reconciling, forgiving, and welcoming.

"No one has made a worse mistake than the one who didn't do anything because he could only do a little."
- Edmund Burke[47] *-*

COMPASSIONATE SERVICE

Survey Questions

Mark the following survey on a scale of 1-10, 1 being a total disagreement, and 10 a total agreement. After finishing your evaluation of all seven phrases, add it up and divide by seven to get a general average for this vital sign. Then consider the questions below.

1. Our church helps people with their physical needs.	
2. Our church helps people find work, clothing, and food as necessary.	
3. Our church provides sufficient training to its members to serve with the community with its needs.	
4. The church has referral agreements with other organizations that can lend practical services to those in need.	
5. The church provides counseling for people who need it.	
6. The people of the community know we want to demonstrate Christ's love in practical ways.	
7. The church works together with community leaders to improve the social context.	

AVERAGE

For Discussion

1. What observations do you have regarding the results of the survey?

2. Which question made you think the most? Why?

3. What one simple step can you take to strengthen this vital sign?

Fourth Function
CARING AND WELCOMING COMMUNITY

Members help each other with their burdens, thus showing the love and compassion of Christ.

"They devoted themselves... to the fellowship...
All the believers were together and had everything
in common... Every day they continued to meet
together... They broke bread in their home and ate
together with glad and sincere hearts"
(Acts 2:42, 44, 46).

The early church understood strength lies in unity. But more than that, people were obeying the prayer of Jesus in which he asked the Father repeatedly to grant unity to the disciples so that the world would believe. The unity of the church is based on the connection between Jesus and the Father. That testimony of unity would constitute the missionary force that moved the church of the first century. That same testimony continues to be the missionary force that pushes today's church.

This unity is superior to the feeling of fraternal love. The early church did not limit itself to a mere passing emotion, but rather it dedicated itself to deep commitment through good and bad times. They voluntarily shared their personal belongings to help the others in the community. This radical, sacrificial love surprised the wider community.

Christians who love each other enjoy being in community—together, united. This is what we call Christian "koinonia." Koinos is a Greek word that means "common." Koinonia, then, means sharing in Christian unity and having things in common. Much of the

Christian life is sharing with others in fraternal love. The important thing is to never forget the missionary purpose of koinonia, as Jesus prayed: "...so that the world may believe that you have sent me" (John 17:21).

If we want the church to grow holistically, we need to recognize the missionary purpose of the Christian community. While community, like service, should be pursued for its own sake, we can never underestimate its impact on the unbelieving world. In a world that suffers isolation, loneliness, separation, and violence, the church provides a community of love, reconciliation, grace, and forgiveness. These qualities, which are difficult to find in other places, contribute to the growth of the Church of the Lord.

Without a doubt, one of the biggest reasons for new converts to join and remain in a congregation is that they feel the fellowship of their brothers and sisters in Christ. If there is no authentic fellowship, people leave and look for alternatives that can satisfy these basic needs that God created in us.

Theologically, we believe God is Triune: Father, Son, and Holy Spirit. They form the first and perfect community—diversity in unity. Man is made in God's image. Therefore, it stands to reason, we are made for community as well! We are designed this way by the Creator. Therefore, the study of church vitality takes seriously not only the evangelization role of the church but also the integration of the person into a true community centered in Christ Jesus. This is demonstrated not only in the love for one another but also in openness to the other and radical hospitality to the world.

"One Another"

It is interesting to note the number of commandments in the New Testament that deal with how people are to treat each other in community. Let's look at some examples.

"Dear friends, let us love ONE ANOTHER..." (1 John 4:7).

"So then, my brothers, when you come together to eat, wait for EACH OTHER..." (1 Corinthians 11:33).

"...So that there should be no division in the body, but that its parts should have equal concern for EACH OTHER" (1 Corinthians 12:25).

"Be kind and compassionate to ONE ANOTHER, forgiving EACH OTHER..." (Ephesians 4:32).

"Submit to ONE ANOTHER out of reverence for Christ" (Ephesians 5:21).

"But encourage ONE ANOTHER daily..." (Hebrews 3:13).

"Therefore confess your sins to EACH OTHER and pray for EACH OTHER..." (James 5:16).

It is evident that the Christian faith should not be lived in solitude or isolated from the brothers and sisters of our community (Hebrews 10:25). Sadly, the entire world is now influenced by individualistic Western culture, a culture that seeks to make us self-sufficient and, with new technologies, isolates us, both through entertainment and faceless communication. The individual spends more time producing and consuming and less time relating to others.

People are made to relate and the worship gatherings should be no exception. It is impressive to note the enormous difference there is between two Christian meetings, one in which people depart as soon as the service has ended, and another where people look for each other, talk, and share. Churches that grow know how valuable it is for the members to have good relationships where they can practice the love and friendship they share in concrete ways. Unfortunately, there are some churches that do many things well, but have this serious problem: they are cold when it comes to expressing love and fellowship among the leaders and the congregants. Church leaders should cultivate the presence of God in our midst, through community, from the launch of the congregation. While we cultivate this characteristic, it is good to be aware that it is God actually doing it!

A Community Ministering Together

Healthy church leadership knows how to incorporate new arrivals adequately into the life of the church. When one is planting a new congregation, the pastor should have thought out what the enfolding process will be for accepting people as members and engaging them in ministry. In trainings for church planters, we have participants write out on a large piece of paper the steps that new people arriving at the church can pass through to mature in the faith and grow until they become leaders. What ministries are there in your church to help Frank and Maria become a part of the work? How will they be received in the congregation? Who will make sure they feel at home? Who will train them? How will they become involved?

Then we ask the leaders to make a diagram, as shown here, with the logical sequence of existing ministries. Later we ask them to identify the gaps where they see they need more ministries. The idea is to have a specific plan to welcome people in with fraternal love and to provide ministries in which they can develop and have a sense of belonging and purpose. Generally speaking, people wait three to six months to find their place in a community of faith, and if they do not find it, they will continue looking elsewhere—or worse, they will grow accustomed to not doing anything besides attending events. It is important to have a clear ministry path that provides a clear process for growth instead of only managing isolated events that are disconnected one from another.

POINTS OF CONTACT	POINTS OF RECEPTION	POINTS OF TRAINING	POINTS OF SERVICE
"Bring a Friend" Event	Intro to Bible Seminar	Women's Bible Study	Deacon
Community Service project	Weekly Worship	Discover Your Gifts Workshop	Children's Ministry
Small Group Friendship	Small Study Group	Ministry Apprenticeship	Community Development

Take a moment to design a diagram to show the steps that would be available in the church that you are planting or leading. Identify the ministries that you need, and ask yourself the following questions:

Do we have sufficient doors of entry for Frank and Maria?

Do we have enough ministries in a logical sequence, so that Frank and Maria can become trained leaders in our church?

What aspects should we improve, based on what we can see in the diagram?

To understand the role that different ministries in the church play in moving a person toward spiritual growth, it is helpful to think in four basic categories:

- **Points of contact**

These are all of the church's ministries, formal or informal, through which the church can enter into contact with people who may be introduced to God and his people. These doors of entry may be special services, concerts, service to the community, or just contact with friends. In the graphic, one can see the different ways people can find entry into the church.

- **Points of Reception**

These are all of the church's ministries, formal or informal, that enfold and incorporate new people into the congregation. If doors of entry are about reaching new people, points of reception are about helping them stick. One might ask, besides the Sunday worship service, what alternatives does the flock have to involve a person in the life of the congregation? Some examples may be a discipleship group, a class on basic doctrine with the pastor, or a shared meal at a member's home. Most of the time, it is about relationships. The content delivered in a group or class is important, but in terms of reception, content is secondary to gaining a sense that "I belong here with these people. I am home." Therefore, hospitality and shared meals are often critical factors in helping new people in the faith find their place.

- Points of Training

These are all the ministries that help people grow in their knowledge of the faith and in their ability to live the Christian life according to biblical principles. They also help people to understand their spiritual gifts and use them for the extension of God's kingdom. Some examples include discipleship classes, small group workshops, guitar classes, conferences on family finances, Bible courses, or preaching classes. Dovetailing with the earlier function of discipleship, the focus is equally on teaching content and training for the Christian life. Sometimes a ministry can serve both as a point of reception and a point of training.

- Points of Service and Ministry

These are all of the ministries that provide positions of service for new believers. It is very important for the church to find places of service and ministry for new members according to their gifts as soon as possible. It could be that a woman prepares food for poor people in the church's kitchen, or a young person could pursue training in how to use the Word to lead Bible studies. It is good to also provide service opportunities for people who might have a physical handicap or are mentally impaired. It is vital to have multiple entry-level points of service so that even those new to the faith have an opportunity to contribute. Next to shared worship and shared meals, a shared task between new members and existing members builds a sense of community more quickly and deeply than almost any other factor. (A shared trial or hardship can create similar bonds, but it is not the type of experience we advocate creating.)

Membership

We have talked about being a caring and welcoming community. People belong to a family as a covenantal community. This manifests itself in people wanting to become members of the local body of Christ. This membership implies certain privileges and responsibilities. Some traditions avoid formal church membership, embracing all who attend worship regularly as members. More frequently, congregations will have formal membership to avoid spiritual drift and clarify commitments to both Christ and his body. Either way, it is important for the church to clearly define expectations for new members and the steps they are expected to follow. In many congregations, people who accept the Lord go through classes of basic doctrine and sign a covenant of commitment when they join the church. Church planter Ralph Moore recommends asking five questions of all who desire to become members of a church:

1. Do you love Jesus Christ and recognize him as Lord of your life and of all creation?
2. Do you respect the leaders of this church and the church's vision?
3. Are you willing to spend time with your new faith family?
4. Do you promise to support the church financially?
5. Are you ready to serve God according to how the Spirit leads you?[48]

Small Group Ministry

One of the greatest tools for creating community is small group ministry. Many churches are recognizing the need to enfold and continue discipling new members through small groups so that they become more mature in the faith and continue to be nourished. A church's capacity to welcome people in fraternal fellowship often determines the church's potential to grow. Small groups (cells or family groups) represent one of the best ways to provide general pastoral care and fellowship. Small groups of Christians provide opportunities to grow spiritually, to experience friendship and fellowship, to get advice, to serve others in times of need, to pray together, and to find support to face the situations of life. Small groups allow for intimacy that leads to mutual trust and deep life sharing, something that does not happen in large groups due to their different nature.

In the New Testament, we find a lot of support for using a strategy of small groups. Jesus focused much of his work and teaching on the 12 disciples. The following passages in the book of Acts show that Christians have met in houses since the first century: 2:46, 5:42, 10:22, 12:12 and 18:26. There were even entire churches that met in houses (Colossians 4:15). Many churches today have also grown by using the advantages of small groups.

Many congregations have discovered the model of CELL-CELEBRATION, which emphasizes small groups in which people are discipled and cared for during the week, then a large-group celebration of praise and worship of God on the weekend or on another agreed-upon date. The church grows when new cells are begun. In addition, the gifts of lay leaders can be used more responsibly, as they can lead the cell groups and foster spiritual growth. A church that operates as a single cell will not grow at the same rate as one that has many small groups, since it depends on only one leader for most of the work and in general does not seek to multiply itself or its leaders.

• Flexibility for scheduling
• Flexibility in meeting location
• Less need for infrastructure (building, furniture, etc.)
• Greater companionship and sense of belonging
• More communication and participation
• More possibilities for intercession
• A better teaching process
• Ability to respond to specific needs
• More personal attention
• Easier development and multiplication of leaders
• Better geographic coverage

What do I do in a Small Group?

There is a significant amount of material and training to promote a very simple but effective agenda for healthy small groups. The agenda presented here is being used successfully in thousands of small groups in Latin America, Africa, Europe, and China. This agenda has some basic steps:

1. Ice breaker

This is a brief, non-threatening activity that is used so that those attending are integrated into the group, participate immediately, and put aside the possible distractions of their daily life. The ice breaker may be an activity in which they learn others' names or everyone shares something--for example, people's favorite foods, interesting anecdotes, or places they have visited. At this time it is not necessary to refer to biblical topics. The principal reason for the ice breaker is for everyone to have a chance to speak during the first few minutes of the meeting. Studies show that this will prompt people to share more openly during the Bible study time.

2. Brief Prayer

Taking into account that those attending may not be familiar with prayer, the prayer should meet three requirements. It should be Audible, Brief, and Christocentric. This is the ABC of prayer. Remember that new people may imitate you in prayer, so the idea is to pray as briefly and simply as possible so that they feel that it is easy and they can do it. It is a big mistake to try to impress people with an extravagant and religious vocabulary. Make the prayer brief and simple.

This could be a recommended prayer to begin the Bible study: "Thank you Lord for this day. We are here to study your Word and we ask that you help us to understand it. Open our minds and our hearts. In the name of Jesus. Amen."

3. Song

Prepare this part ahead of time, choosing a simple song that is easy to learn, or have a way for people to read the words. Be mindful of the new person who does not know these songs.

4. Testimony

Have someone in the group give a brief testimony of God's work in their lives during the week. This will encourage people and provide an environment where they can share a story of what they are learning in their walk with the Lord.

5. Bible Study

This is generally the most important part of the meeting, and it should last half-an-hour to an hour. We recommend that meetings not go more than an hour and a half, so that new people can adjust to this new habit. Meetings that are too long can cause people to leave and not come back. For the study, you might choose a passage of the Bible and do an inductive study of it, or you might choose some appropriate Bible study material such as a denominational series. The length of duration must depend on the cultural circumstances.

6. Intercessory Prayer

Dedicate some time before ending the meeting to pray for each person in the group. This will strengthen the meeting and will build the sense of belonging for those who attend. Remember the prayer requests during the week and ask the participants in later meetings if the Lord has answered their prayers. The simple act of remembering their requests communicates that you are concerned for the members of your small group.

Counseling or Pastoral Care

When a church has small groups, much of the work that a pastor normally has to do is shared among the leaders. Many problems are solved at the level of the small group. The close relationship the members have with their leaders allows for intensive and adequate care among the members of the cell group. This is like the solution Jethro proposed when he told Moses to lighten his workload by dividing it among several leaders at different levels to take care of the diverse matters of the people of Israel (Exodus 18).

Other traditions share the responsibilities for spiritual care and major decisions on behalf of the congregation among a council of elders or deacons. Generally these leaders will take responsibility for segments of the church so that the load is equally shared and the pastor may more freely devote himself to prayer, study, and the welfare of the congregation as a whole.

Whichever model is followed, we should still remember that there are matters with which only pastors or trained counselors should get involved. Cases requiring clinical counseling or involving problems among leaders should be referred to specialists. Every church will face cases requiring counseling; this is why pastoral care and counseling are vital for a growing and strong ministry.

The ministry of pastoral visitation, which allows pastors and leaders to "take the temperature" of the congregation, is also important. Leaders should, from the beginning, train other trustworthy people to carry out follow-up visits.

When the church begins this way, you will not be working against the expectations of people who want only the pastor to visit and won't accept anyone else. In new church plants, the planter can begin making the visits with people to teach them how to do it, and then little by little can give them more responsibility until they can make the visits alone and can even train others. This model, when well organized and supervised, allows for growth in a context of fellowship and harmony among the members.

Conflict in the Community

Every congregation will experience problems at some point in its ministry. A community can appear to be uncaring and unwelcoming due to internal conflicts. When mishandled, conflict can drive people from the church. When handled wisely, conflict can make a congregation stronger. It is likely that all of us have felt some conflict in our lives or witnessed it in our church. The first thing we need to recognize is that conflict is something that is real and normal. Even the apostles experienced conflict (Acts 6 and 15)!

In pastoral training workshops, we sometimes show the leaders a picture of a woman's face and ask them what they see. By the way the picture is composed, some will see an old, ugly woman and others will see a young, beautiful woman. Sometimes they even argue about what the picture shows. Then they realize that what we are trying to illustrate is that the same reality can be seen from different perspectives. As an example, observe the following picture. What did you notice first, the shape of a cup or two faces looking at each other?

Adapted from *Psicología*, Miami: FLET, Unilit, *2002, p. 143.*

Each person has his or her way of seeing things, of working, of communicating. People have their own philosophy of life, values, and priorities. When a lot of people come together, each with a unique perspective, there will certainly be the potential for conflict within the community of faith. No one can deny this. The key lies in the way we deal with conflict. We should try to resolve it in an ethical, constructive, and Christian way.

The first step in resolving conflict is to identify the problem that is causing the conflict. If it can be identified and clearly defined, you've taken a big step towards resolving it. It is not constructive to say the other person is the problem. Both sides should analyze the situation as objectively as possible, trying to reach a solution through clear and effective communication. The purpose is not for one person to win the argument and the other to lose. When things go this way, God's kingdom loses and the enemy rejoices. Let's try to reach an outcome in which everyone wins and God is glorified.

After the problem is identified, follow the pattern of Matthew 18:15-17. We should first talk with our brother or sister in Christ. If the person does not listen, we should return with one or two other brothers or sisters in Christ. If the person still will not listen, we should take the situation before the community of faith.

There are extreme cases in which we find people who refuse to change and who only want to destroy the work of the church. You should treat them with respect and love, but firmly. If, after you've worked to resolve conflicts many times, they continue their destructive and divisive path, you must let them go so that they do not disturb the work and vision of the congregation. Here we see again the importance of communicating the vision of the church clearly, so that there are not misunderstandings about expectations and established goals.

One of the best resources that we have seen on the topic of conflict resolution is *The Peacemaker: A Biblical Guide to Resolving Personal Conflict* by Ken Sande. It contains an excellent biblical foundation as well as practical ideas for implementation in this area. In the following pages, we will present a diagram from the book with biblical explanations on how to resolve conflicts.

In summary, love among brothers and sisters in Christ is one of the most visible testimonies the church will offer in the community. Fellowship and unity are essential qualities that identify the Church of Jesus Christ. The effective church leader remembers the importance of a welcoming and caring community in the church. Where loving God and loving our neighbor are connected, we are free to worship God in spirit and in truth.

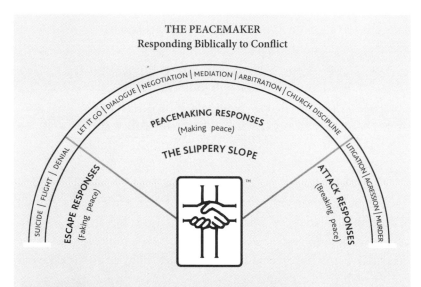

Stay above the Conflict

Conflict can make life very uncomfortable. It takes us by surprise and makes us say or do things that later we will regret. When someone offends us, we can react without thinking. Suddenly it is as if we were sliding down a slippery slope, and things go from bad to worse. As the illustration shows, this slippery slope can make us fall in two directions

1. **ESCAPE RESPONSES.** People tend to use these responses when they are more interested in avoiding a conflict than in resolving it.

    Denial. One way to escape from a conflict is to pretend it not exist. Or, if we cannot deny the problem exists, we simply refuse to do what should be done to resolve a conflict properly. These responses bring only temporary relief and usually make matters worse (see Genesis 16:1-6 and I Samuel 2:22-25).
    Flight. Another way to escape from a conflict is to run away. This may include

leaving the house, ending a friendship, quitting a job, filing for divorce, or changing churches. There may be times when it is appropriate to leave temporarily to calm down, organize your thoughts, and pray. Flight also may be a legitimate response in seriously threatening circumstances (see 1 Samuel 19:9-10), but in most cases running away only postpones a proper solution to a problem.

Suicide. When people lose all hope of resolving a conflict, they make seek to escape the situation by attempting to take their own lives (see 1 Samuel 31:4). Suicide is never the correct way to deal with a conflict.

2. ATTACK RESPONSES. People tend to attack when they are more interested in winning a conflict than in preserving a relationship.

Assault. Some people try to overcome an opponent by using various forms of force or intimidation, such as verbal attacks (including gossip and slander), physical violence, or efforts to damage a person financially or professionally (see Acts 6:8-15). Such conduct always makes conflicts worse.

Litigation. Some conflicts can legitimately be taken before a civil judge (see Romans 13:1-5), but lawsuits usually damage relationships and often fail to achieve complete justice. Also, when Christians are involved on both sides, their witness can be severely damaged. Therefore, it is important for Christians to make every effort to settle a dispute out of court whenever possible (Matthew 5:25-26; I Corinthians 6:1-8).

Murder. In extreme cases, people may be so desperate to win a dispute that they will try to kill those who oppose them (see Acts 7:54-58). While most Christians would not actually kill someone, we should never forget that we stand guilty of murder in God's eyes when we harbor anger or contempt in our hearts toward others (see I John 3:15 and Matthew 5:21- 22).

3. PEACEMAKING RESPONSES. There are six ways we can respond biblically to conflicts and find just solutions to resolve conflicts. We divide them into two types: personal peacemaking and assisted peacemaking.

PERSONAL PEACEMAKING

Overlook an offense. "A man's wisdom gives him patience; it is to his glory to overlook an offense" (Proverbs 19:11). Many disputes can be resolved by quietly overlooking an offense. This is a form of forgiveness and involves a deliberate decision not to talk about it, dwell on it, or let it grow into pent-up bitterness or anger.

Reconciliation. "If your brother has something against you...go and be reconciled (Matthew 5:23-24); if your brother sins against you, go and show him his fault, just between the two of you" (Matthew 18:15a). If an offense is too serious to overlook or has damaged the relationship, we need to resolve personal or relational issues through confession, loving correction, and forgiveness (see Proverbs 28:13 and Galatians 6:1).

Negotiation. "Each one of you should look not only to your own interests, but also to the interests of others" (Philippians 2:4). Questions related to money, property, and other rights should be resolved through a cooperative bargaining process in which you and the other person seek to reach a settlement that satisfies the legitimate needs of each side (Matthew 7:12).

ASSISTED PEACEMAKING

Mediation. "But if he will not listen [to you], take one or two others along..." (Matthew 18:16a). If two people cannot reach an agreement in private, they should ask one or more objective outside people to meet with them to help them communicate more effectively and explore possible solutions. These mediators may ask questions and give advice, but they have no authority to force you to accept a particular solution.

Arbitration. "If any of you has a dispute with another, dare he take it before the ungodly for judgment instead of before the saints?" (1 Corinthians 6:1). When you and an opponent cannot come to a voluntary agreement on a material issue, you may appoint one or more arbitrators to listen to your arguments and render a binding decision to settle the issue.

Church discipline/accountability. "If he refuses to listen to them, tell it to the church..." (Matthew 18:17). If a person who professes to be a Christian refuses to be reconciled and do what is right, the leaders of the church should intervene to promote repentance, justice, and forgiveness.[49]

The four promises of forgiveness

Matthew 6:12; I Corinthians 13:5; Ephesians 4:3

- I will not think any more about this incident.
- I will not mention this incident nor will I use it against you.
- I will not speak with others about this incident.
- I will not let this incident separate us or obstruct our relationship.

"There are many things that you can do alone...but being a Christian is not one of them...The love of brother is inseparable from the love of God."
-William Ham[50]-

CARING AND WELCOMING COMMUNITY

Survey Questions

Mark the following survey on a scale of 1-10, 1 being a total disagreement, and 10 a total agreement. After finishing your evaluation of all seven phrases, add it up and divide by seven to get a general average for this vital sign. Then consider the questions below.

1. The ministry of the church helps members grow in friendly relationship with others.	
2. Visitors and new members are intentionally welcomed into the church.	
3. When someone visits our church, we follow up with them that same week.	
4. Our church has good counseling and pastoral care available for members who need emotional and relational help.	
5. There is a positive fellowship in our church.	
6. Members gather to share a meal or visit each other regularly.	
7. Conflicts in the congregation are resolved biblically.	
AVERAGE	

For Discussion

1. What observations do you have regarding the results of the survey?

2. Which question made you think the most? Why?

3. What one simple step can you take to strengthen this vital sign?

Fifth Function
DYNAMIC WORSHIP AND PRAYER

The church meets as the family of God with the Father in worship, confession, and gratitude, as well as dedicating itself to service and prayer.

"They persevered…in the breaking of bread and in prayer…praising God" (Acts 2:42, 47a).

The first Christians persevered also in the breaking of bread, in prayer, and in praise. A dynamic community like that of the first Christians gets its focus and vitality through worshiping and praising God. The preaching of the Word, as Peter had just finished doing in his first speech after Pentecost, was central. There was also the breaking of bread, the equivalent of what we know today as the Lord's Supper or Communion, within the context of a larger meal. Remembering with the meal what the Lord Jesus Christ had experienced in his death and resurrection, the disciples were spiritually strengthened with the sacrament. They participated in Communion accompanied by a love feast that built community with each other as well as with Christ. Thirdly, through their prayers they were able to center their lives on the most important things without being distracted. Prayer was the lubricant that reduced friction between the brothers and sisters, so that they were able to face opposition, the sword, and even the lions in unity. Prayer included praise, gratitude, confession, and supplication. Prayer also prepared the group for the work of evangelization.

John Stott, in *Signs of The Living Church* (transl. by authors), reminds us that in our worship there should be a balance between formality and informality, between joyfulness and reverence.[51] The church needs to reach a balance between celebration and reverence to keep the worship service centered on the Word. "Celebration," because we Christians have the best reason in the world to celebrate and rejoice in thanks for what Christ has done for us. "Reverence," because we have a God who is not only our friend, but also our King and ruler. When there is a biblical balance, we can celebrate the love of God at the same time that we revere his power and majesty! The church of today needs to give the right balance to praise and worship focused on Christ, to the centrality of biblical preaching and to the teaching of scripture, participation in the sacraments, and to the effective power of prayer if we want to find the dynamism of the early church. Only in this way can we face modern challenges and accomplish the eternal purposes of the Church of Christ.

A church that seeks to grow holistically will foster excellence in worship, both in the Sunday service as well as in other weekly activities that include worship. The place that worship occupies among the functions of the church is primary. When we evangelize or teach, we always have as one of our goals to call for worshipers who worship in spirit and in truth (John 4). Around the entire globe, there has been a great reawakening in Christian worship, especially through music. The church needs well-focused worship to experience healthy and balanced growth.

Worship in Established and Church Planting Contexts

For most of those who study church growth, church health and the missional church, worship is of primary importance in measuring progress in a congregation once it has been established; it is the time when the people of God meet to worship him and listen to his Word. Although worship is not limited to the time or the location of the public worship service, it is at that time that we can measure how certain things are going in the congregation. We observe the level of attendance in the service and we can gauge the level of commitment of the people to being the church gathered. We see the offerings and we can measure how the finances are doing.

We see the number of new visitors and see the results of evangelism. We see those who confess to the Lord, we observe the spirit of worship, and we see many parts of the system functioning at the same time. In *The Church Growth Handbook*, William Easum says that few factors influence church growth as much as the quality of worship. When worship meets people's needs and proves to be a true encounter between God and His people, the church tends to grow.[52]

Worship is also key in church planting. Church planters first begin by making contacts through evangelism, and then they bring together the new converts in Bible study groups, seek commitments from the new believers, and identify and train leaders. Eventually the group begins to hold worship services. In most cases, it is recommended that church planters delay the beginning of worship services until they have consolidated good disciple-making in small groups. However, many people's first contact with a church happens at a corporate worship service. That is why we need to make a good connection. There will never be a second chance to make a first impression! We should consider, therefore, all the details to create an environment that leads to dynamic worship—reverent and celebratory.

Planning Worship

When a pastor wants to start having worship services, one of the best things to do is to establish a planning team. This team designs the services to fulfill the purposes of worship and the proposed worship style. It is great to see how some churches have Bible readings, songs, prayers, and the message synchronized around a particular theme. They then transmit it coherently through all these vehicles of communication. This requires careful planning, but it unleashes amazing creativity. Worship planned by a single individual can be biblical and healthy, but it almost always becomes predictable. Worship planned by a well-orchestrated team is more likely to be fresh and inviting. The worship team would do well to visit other churches with good reputations to see what they can learn and to decide together if there are some ideas they would like to adopt, modify, or consider for their own worship services.

The worship service should be something that elevates and inspires. The worship service teaches, but it also reminds and celebrates. The deepest fiber of our being gets excited when we come before a God who has done marvelous, powerful things in the past, who assures our present, and who guards our certain future. We should be careful not to try to compete with the culture of entertainment and immediate gratification that surrounds us. We should appropriately take advantage of music, poetry, drama, and other artistic means to enrich our liturgy and order of service. Churches have different contexts and cultures that define their flexibility regarding worship. Nevertheless, every church should create a dialogue in worship that includes all of the following points in some responsible way:

- God calls us to worship. The congregation of believers responds with jubilation.
- God calls us to repentance. All respond by confessing in prayer.
- God speaks through his Word. The community of faith responds with songs and offerings.
- God gives his blessing. The body responds by going out to serve.

The Style of the Worship Service

Many factors affect the type of worship churches choose. For example, some emphasize more the transcendental nature of God (his greatness and how much greater he is than we are) and others the immanence of God (his identification and closeness to human beings). It is good to have a balance between the two poles and to emphasize the different aspects according to the different times in the church year. It enriches the experience of a worship service when there are a variety of approaches to the liturgical act. For example, a worship service on Good Friday should have a very different tone from one on Easter Sunday. Perhaps a service on Good Friday should be more somber to create an expectation for the celebration that will come on Easter. The celebration of Christmas will be very different from a service that emphasizes confession of sin and repentance. In the same way that the Scriptures contain an immense variety of literary styles, so too our worship services should look to fill and provide, in time, the biggest range of healthy and biblical experiences. *The important thing is to remember that the style of ministry emanates from the church's mission and vision as informed and shaped by the mission of God.*

In the following diagram, we offer a tool useful for analyzing your church's own style and emphasis and for discussing it with others who participate in your church planting team. If you wish, you can put numbers from 1-5 on the categories. Then have each participant rank their opinion with a number and share the results with the group, explaining their perspectives. For example, this person circled number 2 because he believes the atmosphere of the worship service is somewhat celebrative.

Example:

Celebrative	**ATMOSPHERE**	Somber
1	←—②——— 3 ———4—→	5

When this tool is used, remember there is no one right answer. For example, there will be worship services in which the focus is completely on deep discipleship for believers. But there will be other services, such as "Bring Your Friend" day, in which the focus will be on reaching nonbelievers. The idea is to create a church identity that is in agreement with the church's vision.

Spontaneous	**PLANNING**	Detailed
1	←—2——— 3 ———4—→	5

Exciting	**EMOTION**	Reserved
1	←—2——— 3 ———4—→	5

Little	**VARIETY**	A lot
1	←—2——— 3 ———4—→	5

Low	**PARTICIPATION**	High
1	←—2——— 3 ———4—→	5

Low	**TECHNOLOGY**	High
1	←—2——— 3 ———4—→	5

Nonbelievers	**FOCUS**	Believers
1	←—2——— 3 ———4—→	5

Traditional	**MUSIC**	Contemporary
1	←—2——— 3 ———4—→	5

Intellectual		**PREACHING**		Emotional
1	←2—	3	—4→	5

Little		**MINISTERING**		A lot
1	←2—	3	—4→	5

Public		**RESPONSE**		Private
1	←2—	3	—4→	5

Open		**VISITORS**		Closed
1	←2—	3	—4→	5

Individual		**LEADERSHIP**		Team
1	←2—	3	—4→	5

Liturgical		**PROTOCOL**		Informal
1	←2—	3	—4→	5

Celebratory		**ATMOSPHERE**		Somber
1	←2—	3	—4→	5

Questions about worship styles:

- How do we view the worship style we currently use?
- What aspects do we like about our worship style?
- What aspects do we want to change or modify?
- What would we have to do to make these changes?

The Worship Service and the Culture

When traveling to different continents, one quickly notices that worship can look very different from place to place. Some may ask how this can be, when we have the same God and the same Bible. The answer has to do with the fact that all worship occurs within a local culture. All belief and theology travels through a particular language and culture. The Lutheran World Federation Nairobi Statement on Worship and Culture proposes a framework that is helpful in understanding some of these meaningful aspects of worship.[53]

Worship should be…

Contextual: In the same way Christ humbled himself (Philippians 2) and identified himself with humanity in the form of a Jewish baby, people express their worship of God within their particular cultural context identifying with the local environment. All cultures of the world can worship God. Any elements and values of a culture that are in harmony with the gospel, can glorify God in worship. Anita Stauffer, in *Christian Worship: Unity in Cultural Diversity*, explains that contextualization of the gospel is necessary for it to build deep roots in local cultures.[54] A classic example is the use in Andean countries of musical instruments called the *charango* and the *bombo* to praise God. Some of the first missionaries said that these were instruments of the devil and that they were not for use in the worship of the church. Thanks be to God, today the gospel is more contextualized and there are thousands of praise groups using folk instruments. Which aspects of your worship service reflect your cultural context?

Countercultural: In the same way that Christ turned over the tables of the vendors who were profaning the temple with their avarice and called the Pharisees a "brood of vipers," worship of God is expressed by confronting the aspects of the culture that go against the values of the gospel. Jesus Christ came to transform all cultures. The Word calls us not to conform to this world, but to be transformed by the renewing of our minds (Romans 12). Therefore, the worship service should reflect the culture but also confront it. The biblical and prophetic elements of worship, such as calls to repentance, to justice, and to social and community conscience, need to recur in our worship services. What are the aspects of our culture we should reject? In what ways does our worship service help us to remember we are a different people?

Cross-cultural & Multi-cultural: The book of Revelation (5:9; 7:9) shows us that there will be people from every language, tribe, and nation in the kingdom of God. Jesus came to be the savior of every nation and not of just one while excluding others. In the Old and New Testaments, we have ample evidence that the message of God crosses all types of barriers and borders. There is only one Lord, only one baptism, and only one gospel. However, there are different cultural expressions of this reality. Our worship service can also reflect the universality of the gospel and can make use of art, music, architecture, customs, and values of other cultures to enrich the liturgical act. How do we express the universality and intercultural nature of the gospel in our church?

Transcultural: In the same way the resurrection of Christ demonstrates a power and truth that goes beyond our understanding and culture, the worship service also reflects something beyond one or even the sum of all cultures. The gospel has supracultural aspects. The triune God and all his works (creation, redemption, sanctification, etc.) exceed human comprehension and take us beyond the possibility that any one culture or even all cultures together could express faith completely or perfectly. The element of mystery in the Christian faith should also have a place in our worship services. The Word says that even the peace of God "transcends all understanding" (Philippians 4:7), and 2 Peter 1:4 says, "...He has given us his very great and precious promises, so that through them you may participate in the divine nature and escape the corruption in the world caused by evil desires." Without falling into the error of the New Age movement, which says that each human being is a god, we should understand that the Christian faith allows us to be collaborators with God, and it offers much more than the world could ever understand or appreciate. What aspects of our worship help us to connect with a God that transcends every human culture?

WORSHIP AND CULTURE

TRANSCULTURAL
Reflects the mystery of faith
that goes beyond the
sum of all cultures

COUNTERCULTURAL
Confronts culture in a
biblical and prophetic way

CROSSCULTURAL
Learns from and is enriched by
the crossing of borders

CONTEXTUAL
Identifies with the culture,
seeking its transformation

FINAL PURPOSE: *TRANSFORMATION OF THE CULTURE*

Adapted from the Nairobi Declaration by John Wagenveld

Church leaders who take these four elements of the relationship between worship and culture into account will enrich the worship experience of the people with whom they work. The most important thing is for the worship service to reflect that God is alive, present, and in communion with his people. This will help in reaching the desired end: that through the experience of worship, the worshipers will leave to *transform* their culture for Christ.

Many of the controversies regarding worship are nothing more than arguments about likes and temperament. In reality, there is a place for a wide variety of expressions of worship in the rich diversity of the Church of the Lord. As Hesselgrave says, "True Christian worship is first and foremost the honoring of God as God, and the ascription of praise and thanksgiving to him for what he is and has done."[55]

Basic Considerations

The welcome visitors and congregants receive to the worship service is essential. This is the important part of the ushers' ministry, as they welcome people with a smile and with a desire to serve. They give people the bulletin, if there is one, and make sure that those who are attending for the first time receive a card on which they can write down their contact information. Give these cards to the pastor, so that depending on the culture, the pastor can introduce the visitors during the service or personally greet them afterwards. Some cultures will handle the rapport with the visitor differently, but the key is to have some way to get to know the people and offer hospitality. Remember that many first time visitors decide that day if they will return to the worship service or not; therefore, receive them well. We should make every effort so the visitor feels the warmth of the Christian community and hears clearly the good news of salvation Christ offers. We encourage you to create a follow-up team to make a timely contact with every new visitor.

The follow-up team is responsible for recognizing and taking advantage of each opportunity to find a date to visit the new attendees. If possible, it is good to send a note or make a telephone call to the new people, showing sincere interest in them and inviting visitors back to worship together. When John began Principe de Paz (Prince of Peace) Church, there was a couple who said that what impressed them the most was that they were visited 24 hours after their first telephone call. Follow-up is like the motor of an airplane— without it you cannot take off.

Another consideration is the size of the sanctuary and the number of seats that are available. Sadly, many meeting places are built with very little vision for the future. Some churches limit their growth indefinitely because their buildings are too small or their property has no room for expansion. They choke off their growth before they even begin. When people arrive at a place that is nearly full, they feel squeezed and begin to be uncomfortable. When a congregation reaches 80 percent of its seating capacity, it should consider the options to enlarge its capacity: adding services, expanding the meeting place, or moving to a bigger location. Many churches that add services experience significant growth in the first months after the change. Do not let the lack of space stifle the growth of your worshiping community.

Biblical, solid preaching is essential for a healthy church. The messages should reach both the head and the heart. Challenges from the pulpit should be applicable to daily life and should strengthen today's family with healthy doctrine. Always craft your message, and the entire service, on the assumption that you are addressing at least one long term Christian and one person exploring the faith for the first time. Dedicate time to design good messages that address the needs of the people, and that over time provide the teachings of the whole Bible. Malphurs reminds us, "While there are many people who are interested in the details of the end of the world, there are many more who are interested in knowing how they can make it to the end of the week!"[56] Look for a balance between the practical and the conceptual, and use many illustrations and stories to communicate the principles you are teaching in an interesting way. Watch the time, and with few exceptions, end in a positive way that communicates grace and hope in Jesus.

Adapt the program to your liturgical style, and encourage and urge people to take steps of faith in response to the spiritual transformation that God is carrying out in them. People appreciate challenges to action and opportunities to respond to the call of God. The answer to the call may be private or public. It is also good to provide opportunities so that during the course of the service (before, during, or after), people who desire prayer for special needs can come to the front or go to a special room where someone can accompany them in prayer.

Promote participation by the leaders and the members of the flock. Use their talents and gifts for the edification of the body during the worship service. The worship leaders are key people. They should be mature people, respected, having a good testimony, and they should be worshippers who want to lead others in the worship of God. Music is one of the areas in which a good number of people can be involved. Depending on how the church grows, the leadership can foster the creation of new musical groups: children's, youth, and adult choirs, orchestras, or special bands. Take care that the words of the music communicate biblical truths and do not conflict with what you are teaching. As you involve more people, according to their gifts, church attendance will continue to improve.

Make use of the testimonies of people who have known the grace, mercy, and transforming love of God. The greatest challenge will be making sure the focus remains on God and not on them. Testimonies have a subtle way of twisting the spotlight to shine on either "how bad I was" or "how good I've become" rather than shining on the transformative power of God. Nevertheless, it is important to let people share their spiritual pilgrimages in public for the edification of everyone. When others see what God is doing in the community, it is contagious and they begin showing interest in participating and contributing to the work.

Baptism and the Lord's Supper

The sacraments are an integral part of the worship service. Church planters should read books and literature that their denomination recommends to learn the theology and practice of baptism and the Lord's Supper. Teaching should accompany the sacraments. Leaders should also know the varied forms of ritual (in the good sense of the word) permitted in the local context. But beyond protocol, church planters should know how to create meaningful experiences that deepen believers' faith and open opportunities to give testimony with these sacraments.

Baptism provides an excellent opportunity to celebrate the entry of a new believer into the family of faith, to explain its importance, and to call those who have not yet taken that step. It is even better when this ceremony can be accompanied by a testimony. With the Lord's Supper, there is also an opportunity to explain the profound meaning of the work of Jesus and the communion of the saints that this work makes possible. Avoid falling into routines: experiment with different forms that fulfill the same function within biblical parameters. If you are limited to one way of administering the Lord's Supper, enrich the occasion with different biblical metaphors, relevant sermons, and music that focuses on this special event.

Prayer

Practical Steps

1. Begin a discipline of personal prayer in private.
2. Find prayer intercessors to support you.
3. Pray regularly with the leaders of the church in small groups.
4. Develop a prayer ministry in the entire church.

Let's highlight some relevant points. First, prayer reminds us daily that the work belongs to God and not to us. Our prayer, confession, requests, and petitions assure that the solid base on which the church is built is the triune and true God. By putting the brakes on our activity and stopping ourselves to pray, we recognize that we depend on divine grace and we do not rely on our own understanding nor our own strength. One pastor said, "If we are to prevail over men in public, we must prevail with God in private."

Second, prayer is the lubricating oil that allows all the "machinery" to work well. The machine not maintained with oil soon becomes rusty and useless. The same thing happens with the church that does not pray. We should center ourselves on God's will, bathing all the ministries in prayer, seeking the presence of God, so that he blesses our efforts. Poetically we may say, "Prayer moves the hand of God." However, in reality, prayer does not change God as much as it changes us!

Third, prayer unites the leaders and the congregation. It is difficult for conflicts, anger, jealousy, disagreements, and annoyances to take root in the soil of people's hearts watered constantly with prayer. We do not know a better activity to unite a team than praying together. Prayer maintains the harmony between brothers and sisters. Prayer unifies and maintains us in the will of the Lord. As a colleague says, "Prayer keeps you far from sin and sin keeps you far from prayer."

Fourth, prayer strengthens the church to reach out to the community. Saturate all evangelistic projects with prayer. We need to be under the protective hand of God, centered in the love of Christ, and wrapped with the impulsive energy of the Holy Spirit when going out as ambassadors of the Lord. Nevertheless, it is not enough to talk. We should work at it, put it into practice. Richard Pratt, in *Pray with Your Eyes Open*, mentions how the prayer retreats that he has experienced have been full of discussion and planning. He says prayer meetings often end up being about many things other than actually praying.[57]

A church's practice of prayer is usually a reliable indicator of the spiritual level of a church. The absence of prayer characterizes a stagnant or sick church. This Christian discipline can be the contagious spark that starts the biblical fire in the hearts of lifeless people and that shines the way for those who are wandering on mistaken paths.

In some ways, prayer is the beginning of all ministry and worship is its chief end. Together, as bookends, they invigorate all the other aspects of holistic ministry mentioned in this book. Evangelism, discipleship, service, and fellowship can all come together in the acts of prayer and worship, which nurtures us to keep on with the task. At the same time, we simply accept prayer and worship as gifts from the Lord. His gift to us becomes our task.

"Missions is not the ultimate goal of the Church. Worship is. Missions exists because worship doesn't."
- John Piper [58]*-*

DYNAMIC WORSHIP AND PRAYER

Survey Questions

Mark the following survey on a scale of 1-10, 1 being a total disagreement, and 10 a total agreement. After finishing your evaluation of all seven phrases, add it up and divide by seven to get a general average for this vital sign. Then consider the questions below.

1. The worship in our church nurtures and strengthens us for the Christian life.	
2. The music used in services helps the congregation experience the living presence of God.	
3. The messages preached are appreciated by the congregation.	
4. Our worship services attract youth.	
5. I feel comfortable inviting a friend or relative to church.	
6. Looking at the whole worship experience, I feel satisfied overall.	
7. In our worship services the triune God is recognized: Father, Son and Holy Spirit.	

AVERAGE

For Discussion

1. What observations do you have regarding the results of the survey?

2. Which question made you think the most? Why?

3. What one simple step can you take to strengthen this vital sign?

CONCLUSION

To summarize, in these two sections we have briefly analyzed the ten vital signs of a healthy church. This framework helps us to know what we are aiming toward when we seek to establish a healthy new congregation or revitalize an existing one. It is good to start this process with a clear picture in our mind. What are we working toward? What should the church we want to plant look like? What are the vital ingredients of a healthy church? This is how we begin: with the end in mind.

We examined the five basic commitments that should be present in any church, and then we reviewed the five functions of its ministry. When planting a church, you can use this framework as a starting point for organization, planning, and evaluation. It should be clear these ten areas should not be merely static, but rather they should be understood as commitments to be developed dynamically and effectively according to the particular context.

Now that we have described the vital functions of the church, take a moment to do the following exercise. We recommend that you do it alone on a piece of paper first, and then share it with a small study group or with the leaders with whom you work. Compare your results. Then summarize the contributions of the entire group on a large sheet of paper. It is good to first list all the ministries that are currently functioning, and then list the ministries that you hope to begin and develop.

THE FIVE VITAL FUNCTIONS PLANNING TOOL

Take the five vital functions of the church separately, and make a list of the ministries that fall under each function. Every six months, revise the list to see where you need to make adjustments.

WITNESS	DISCIPLESHIP	SERVICE	COMMUNITY	WORSHIP

Remember that there is not just one way of doing things and that no list can satisfy all the requirements of a given situation. What we propose here is a good framework to use as a starting point, taking into account the Word of God and the experience of the church and those who went before us. The important thing is to focus on all of these ideas from God's perspective, in such a way that the total ministry is missional and seeks the edification of the body of Christ so that it works for his glory and the expansion of his mission through the multiplication of disciples and healthy churches.

Reproducing the church

The good thing about church planting is that the five functions reproduce themselves again and again with new congregations. Each church has the responsibility to multiply these functions in new disciples and, when possible, in new churches. Once a brother in Christ in Nicaragua told us that we were missing a function. He said that function was reproduction, and he was right. We need to be reproducing these functions constantly, and one of the best ways to do this is to plant new churches. If we have a fruit tree, taking very good care of it will help it produce more fruit, but it can only grow so big. If we want to produce more fruit, it is better to use the seeds of some of the fruit to plant new trees that will produce their own fruit. Some churches have grown to very impressive sizes, but the size of the mother church does not come close to the numbers of people reached and leaders produced by all the daughter churches that have been planted.

According to Ralph Moore, a church planter in Hawaii and the founder of a movement that has launched hundreds of churches around the world, there are three fundamental impediments to church reproduction that need alternative and creative solutions to be overcome. These are the following limiting expectations:

1. Formal training in a theological seminary for pastors
2. A building dedicated to worship services
3. A pastor who is employed full-time

Moore recommends training pastors locally and sending them to Bible institutes or seminaries only after they have begun a church, or providing theological education without removing them from their place of work. Secondly, he suggests that churches rent or borrow a meeting space for several years before purchasing or constructing a building. He says buildings tend to shape the thinking of the church planter and the growing congregation and often limit the potential growth. Thirdly, he recommends churches begin with bivocational pastors (ones who have a secular job to earn a salary), an approach that has many advantages, as long as the weaknesses of this model, such as tiredness, lack of family time, and the need to establish credibility, are considered.[59]

The key question is, therefore: When you lead a church, will you instill in it the vision for reproducing the vital functions of the church by planting other daughter churches?

We conclude reiterating what we wrote in the preface, which provides a unifying anchor to the book. The ten indicators or vital signs of a healthy community of faith are rooted in the character and nature of God. The healthy church understands its mission and purpose in the world and organizes its life and work to be faithful and effective in its given context.

It is our prayer that these 10 vital signs will help you have some healthy conversations as you seek to carry out your calling as a congregation in mission to the world. Grounded in the Scriptures and led by the Spirit the community of faith can avoid the extremes of "churchless mission" and "missionless church" to have an integrated approach to be a signpost of the Kingdom of God.

"God's use of power is demonstrated supremely on the cross. There Satan used his full might to destroy Christ, or to provoke him to use his divinity wrongly. Either would have meant defeat for Christ—the first because Satan would have overcome him and the second because it would have destroyed God's plan of salvation. Godly power is always rooted in love, not pride; redemption, not

revenge; and concern for the other, not self. It is humble,
not proud, and inviting, not rejecting. Its symbol is the
cross, not the sword. This is why the world sees God's
power as weakness (1 Cor. 1:23-27)."
-- Hiebert, Shaw and Tienou[60] *--*

"The call of the gospel is for the church to implement
the victory of God in the world through suffering love.
The cross is not just an example to be followed; it is an
achievement to be worked out, put into practice. But it is
an example nonetheless, because it is the exemplar—the
template, the model—for what God now wants to do by his
Spirit in the world, through his people. It is the start of the
process of redemption, in which suffering and martyrdom
are the paradoxical means by which victory is won."
--N.T. Wright[61]*--*

Next step

You can now take the scores from the survey you took after each chapter and put those on to the following chart so you have it all on one page. Then, if you follow the instructions in the Appendix, you can process this information as a congregation to continue some healthy conversations about your life and mission as a church.

	VITAL ELEMENTS					VITAL FUNCTIONS				
	VISION	LEADERSHIP	MOBILIZED BODY	RESOURCES	TEXT AND CONTEXT	EVANGELISM	EDUCATION & DISCIPLESHIP	SERVICE	FELLOWSHIP	WORSHIP
1										
2										
3										
4										
5										
6										
7										
TOTAL ADD										
DIVIDE	7	7	7	7	7	7	7	7	7	7
NUMBER OF QUESTIONS										
EQUAL										
AVERAGE										

GRAPH YOUR RESULTS HERE

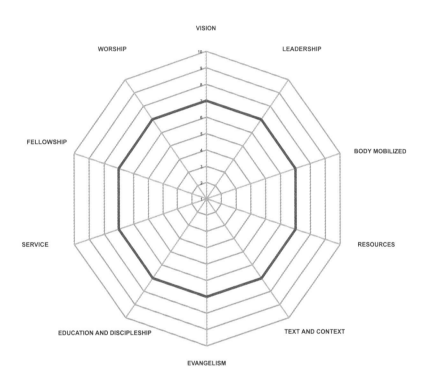

SAMPLE RESULTS OF
COMMUNITY CHURCH

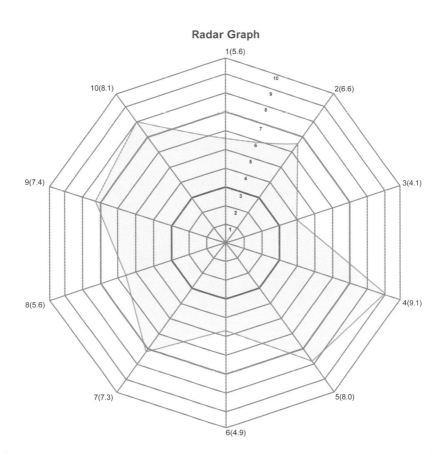

Radar Graph

VITAL KEY COMMITMENTS OF
THE HEALTHY CHURCH

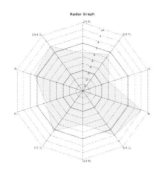

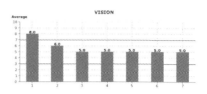

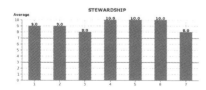

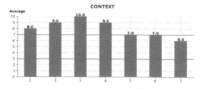

VITAL KEY FUNCTIONS OF
THE HEALTHY CHURCH

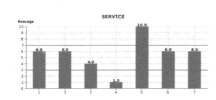

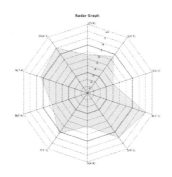

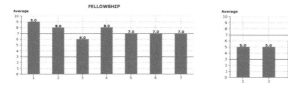

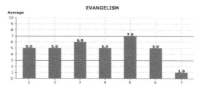

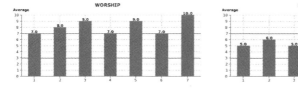

APPENDIX

INTRODUCTION

TAKE YOUR CHURCH'S PULSE is an instrument that can help you diagnose your congregation's health by evaluating several key areas of church life. It serves as a tool for self-evaluation and planning in the local church, two important processes for churches that seek both quantitative and qualitative growth. This tool is provided free of charge by the Multiplication Network, an organization that promotes healthy church development and fosters the establishment of new churches around the world.

In addition to serving as a measuring instrument that reveals vital information about the state of a congregation's health, the purpose of TAKE YOUR CHURCH'S PULSE is to encourage dialogue and deep reflection among leaders, members, and pastors of local churches regarding the important elements that determine a congregation's development and health. This tool is only worth the healthy conversation that it engenders among leaders who seek to make prayerful changes led by the Holy Spirit to be a better witness for the kingdom of God in their community.

The following ten characteristics are described in the book Take Your Church's Pulse. They are divided into two groups: five key commitments and five vital functions.

5 KEY COMMITMENTS	5 VITAL FUNCTIONS
A clear and inspiring vision	Compelling witness
A mobilizing leadership	Comprehensive discipleship
A motivated ministering body	Compassionate service
Proper stewardship of resources	Caring and welcoming community
Integration of text and context	Dynamic worship and prayer

GENERAL RECOMENDATIONS FOR THE USER

This is a process rather than an activity.

This tool is only as valuable as the discussion that it generates. The central idea is that TAKE YOUR CHURCH'S PULSE can help leaders to direct their conversations, first in evaluation and then in planning, for the purpose of building a more effective ministry that will result in a healthier church. Remember that this tool is the BEGINNING of a process and that changes do not happen overnight. The facilitator should remind the group that this is a process that takes time—it is not just a one-time activity.

The questionnaire should be filled out by as many church members as possible.

This instrument works best if most of the people belonging to the congregation (members or regular attendees) fill out the form and turn it in so that the leaders can evaluate the results. Congregants can fill out the forms anonymously if they prefer. The leaders should calculate the averages and list any participants' additional written comments. The greater the number of members/attendees who fill out the questionnaires, the more representative and useful will be the information the leadership group has available.

The form should be filled out by all of the leaders who participate in the process.

The leaders should also fill out the form, but we suggest they not do it anonymously, since they will have to present their point of view throughout the process of analysis, evaluation, and interpretation. The average scores from the leadership group should be calculated and then compared to the average scores from the congregation. Sometimes the differences between the leadership and the congregation are notable, and it may be very helpful to list them, analyze them, and discuss them. There is no exact rule for the size of the evaluation group, but we suggest that it include between 5 and 15 leaders.

The spirit of the process should be constructive.

This exercise should be accompanied by prayer, and it should take place in an atmosphere of emotional and spiritual maturity, where everyone feels safe to share opinions freely. The strengths and weaknesses of the church need to be discovered. Leaders tend to celebrate strengths, but they should also be open to recognizing the weak areas of the church so that these can be strengthened.

RECOMMENDED STEPS

1. Explore – Download a copy of the survey and examine the questions to ensure that the tool will fit your congregation. The vital signs Take Your Church's Pulse identifies are important ones but are not the only factors your congregation needs to consider. The questions in it may also make assumptions you

don't want to make. Before you begin, make sure your leaders are comfortable that the survey will measure the factors you are interested in. A digital copy of the survey can be downloaded from www.multiplicationnetwork.org under Training Materials. All the tools there are free but require that you sign in (also free).

2. Agree – Secure agreement from your church leadership to do this project. It is important that there be a clear understanding of process and a commitment to follow it through. (There is an optional Strategic Planning Guide that offers some additional help in getting the most out of the tool, which is also found at www.multiplicationnetwork.org/training-materials/, but it is often more complex than many churches want to get into. Simply use the parts you like.)

3. Sign up – Have your pastor go to www. multiplicationnetwork. org and click on the Take Your Church's Pulse logo. You will be redirected to www.edutecnologia.org/pulse/index. php?lang=en. There you will be given the option to download a pdf of the survey so you can print and copy it so your congregation can do it on paper or option 2: the pastor will be able to sign your church up to do the survey online. This option will automatically tally and graph your results for you. The pastor will be sent the appropriate links in an email, one for the survey and another for the results.

4. Share the Survey link with your leadership team and have them fill it out first. These results will offer a baseline for comparison with the congregation as a whole and help determine if the leadership and congregation are on the same page.

5. Share the Survey link with your congregation and give them a deadline for participating. For the less technologically inclined, paper copies can be provided, filled out and collected and then the data can be entered by a member with computer skills.

6. Examine the results as a leadership team and review the process for discussion as a congregation. Now that you have the results of your survey, there are four valid strategies for selecting priorities for your goals:

- **The Barrel and Staves** – A barrel is constructed of multiple staves. If you try to fill a barrel with water, it will fill only to the lowest stave. At that point, instead of climbing any higher, the water will run out. Our weaknesses can create back doors to our churches, causing existing members to exit as quickly as new members enter. If that is the case, often the quickest path to growth is addressing our weaknesses in order to retain the people we have. If, as you look at your survey results, you see weaknesses that are crippling your ministry and will prevent your gifts from ever reaching their full potential, that may be your place to begin.

- **Leading with Your Gifts** – Just as individual members have spiritual gifts, so too congregations have particular strengths. Rather than trying to become someone else's ideal congregation, focus on being the congregation God intended you to be by identifying your unique gifts and putting them to work. Often our fully exploited strengths are more valuable to the kingdom of God than our marginally improved weaknesses. Plus, it is often easier to move a strength by 2 points than it is to move a weakness 1 point. If you have a strong, clear sense of vision and giftedness, playing to your strengths is a good choice, though you may wish to tackle one weaker area as a secondary goal to strengthen your ministry platform.

- **The Tennis Racquet** – The Spider-web graph often reminds people of the face of a tennis racquet. With most sport equipment, from baseball bats to golf clubs to a soccer player's foot, there is a "sweet spot," which, when making contact with the ball, gives you both the most power and the most control. With a tennis racquet, if you expand the size of the racquet face, you increase your sweet spot. Your spider-web graph shows the sweet spot of your church, the size of your ministry effectiveness. Instead of worrying about strengths or weaknesses, look for ways to maximize your sweet spot. If you could move one or two of your factors 1 point further out on the scale, which factors would increase the size of your sweet spot most quickly? The tennis racquet approach is always healthy as it will constantly be challenging you to broaden your ministry in new directions. If you can't decide between the approaches, it is a safe place to start.

- **The Snowball Approach** – When a little snowball begins rolling down the mountain, it collects more and more snow on its outer surface. As it rolls, it grows in size, in speed, in weight and in power until it is mowing down the trees in its path. The secret is in starting small and building momentum as you go. If your congregation has little positive momentum at present, often it is most helpful to choose small obtainable goals where you can get an "easy win." This will build confidence to tackle more challenging goals in the future. The snowball approach is particularly helpful to ministries who have experienced a setback, a blow to their morale, or who have been plateaued for a long while. Momentum is a powerful tool. Use it to make your ministry more effective for the Kingdom. After reviewing your survey results, simply decide which one or two areas could give your church a quick and easy win.

7. Share the results with the congregation and have a larger discussion. Often the results will simply confirm what you already know intuitively. It is often the discussion about the results where the greatest value is found. It fosters unity and creativity. Christ's promise in Matthew 18:19-20 frequently proves true: "I tell you that if two of you on earth agree about anything they ask for, it will be done for them by my Father in heaven. For where two or three gather in my name, there am I with them." Christ shows up and his heart for the church becomes apparent as the members discuss together how to best follow him.

8. Decide next steps for your church's future. We advise narrowing it down to two strategic goals to focus on over the next 3-5 years. With that kind of focus, many times the goals are achieved ahead of schedule creating an opportunity for celebration and an eagerness to take on the next challenge. If you have to establish more goals, prioritize them and rank them 1, 2, 3… Put them on the agenda for each leadership meeting to make sure they don't get lost in the shuffle of everyday ministry.

WHO SHOULD FACILITATE THIS PROCESS?

There are several options for facilitating the process.

1. The first option is for the pastor or a leader assigned by the church's board of directors to provide the necessary leadership to direct the self-evaluation process. It is very important that the person be respected by the members of the group. The principal task of the facilitator should be to moderate the discussion, assuring that everyone can participate and that the process does not go off track. Some pastors prefer someone else moderate the process so that they can be a more active and independent participant in the discussion.

2. The second option is to communicate with a trainer from the Multiplication Network (find the representative closest to you on the web page www.multiplicationnetwork.org) so that they can help your group with the analytical process. Generally this option would take place in the context of a retreat, and the participants would be assigned to continue the process with their own leadership group.

POSSIBLE PROBLEMS

Conflicts and antagonistic individuals

When a variety of different viewpoints arise in a self-evaluation such as this one, it can generate conflict, and the group must be prepared to manage conflict in a healthy way. Conflict should not be avoided, but people must know how to channel it in a positive and constructive manner. The process should not be allowed to get off track by discussing a single point extensively or by permitting one antagonistic person to dominate the entire discussion. The constructive purpose of the evaluation must be remembered.

WARNING:

This tool is designed to be used in a positive, harmonious, and constructive context for the purpose of helping to improve the local church. It is not designed to be used in hostile or toxic environments; there are other resources for those types of situations that go much deeper than this tool. Churches that are experiencing large divisions or grave conflicts, or churches in which the local pastor feels very threatened by the evaluation process, should look for other types of help if they wish to undertake this kind of process.

CHARACTERISTICS OF THIS TOOL

To make the information from the survey easy to access and interpret, the online version is expressed graphically. For each vital sign there is a bar graph for each question to enable the user to quickly identify highs and lows. There is a similar graph for all of the signs. These graphs utilize the common point scale from 1 to 10, where 10 represents total agreement with the descriptive phrase and 1 represents complete disagreement.

1 to 2	This is a very low grade and represents **strong disagreement** with the criterion used to evaluate some aspect of the church.
3 to 4	This is a low grade and represents **moderate disagreement** with the criterion used to evaluate some aspect of the church.
5 to 6	These are middle scores that can indicate a medium grade, or, in a few cases, a **neutral position** on the subject being evaluated.
7 to 8	This is a high grade, and it represents **moderate agreement** with the criterion used to evaluate some aspect of the church.
9 to 10	This is an excellent grade that represents **strong agreement** with the criterion used to evaluate some aspect of the church.

DEFINITIONS OF CHURCH

FROM DIFFERENT DENOMINATIONAL TRADITIONS

SOUTHERN BAPTIST CONVENTION

A New Testament church of the Lord Jesus Christ is an autonomous local congregation of baptized believers, associated by covenant in the faith and fellowship of the gospel, observing the two ordinances of Christ, governed by his laws, exercising the gifts, rights, and privileges invested in them by his Word, and seeking to extend the gospel to the ends of the earth.

www.sbc.org/bfm/bfm2000.asp#vi

ASSEMBLIES OF GOD

We believe 'the Church' is the body of Christ and consists of the people who, throughout time, have accepted God's offer of redemption (regardless of religious denomination) through the sacrificial death of his son Jesus Christ. The church has a mission to seek and save all who are lost in sin.

ag.org/top/Beliefs/Statement_of_Fundamental_Truths/sft_short.cfm

GENERAL ASSOCIATION OF GENERAL BAPTISTS

We believe that the Church universal is the body of Christ, the fellowship of all believers, and that its members have been called out from the world to come under the dominion and authority of Christ, its head. We believe that a local church is a fellowship of Christians, a part of the body of Christ, voluntarily banded together for worship, nurture, and service.

http://www.generalbaptist.com/#/identity/statements-of-faith

UNITED CHURCH OF CHRIST

From the United Church of Christ statement of faith:
God bestows upon us the Holy Spirit, creating and renewing the Church of Jesus Christ, binding in covenant faithful people of all ages, tongues, and races. God calls us into the church to accept the cost and joy of discipleship, to be servants in the service of the whole human family, to proclaim the gospel to all the world and resist the powers of evil, to share in Christ's baptism and eat at his table, to join Him in his passion and victory.

http://www.ucc.org/beliefs/statement-of-faith.html

ORTHODOX PRESBYTERIAN CHURCH

Christ has established his church, and particular churches, to gather and perfect his people, by means of the ministry of the Word, the sacraments of baptism (which is to be administered to the children of believers, as well as believers) and the Lord's supper (in which the body and blood of Christ are spiritually present to the faith of believers), and the disciplining of members found delinquent in doctrine or life. Christians assemble on the Lord's day to worship god by praying, hearing the word of god read and preached, singing psalms and hymns, and receiving the sacraments.

http://www.opc.org/beliefs.html

MARS HILL CHURCH

We believe that the Church, which is the body and espoused bride of Christ, is a spiritual organism made up of all born–again persons (Eph. 1:22, 23; 5:25–27; 1 Cor. 12:12–14; 2 Cor.11:2). We believe that the establishment and continuance of local churches is clearly taught and defined in the New Testament Scriptures (Acts 14:27, 18:22, 20:17; 1 Tim. 3:1–3; Titus 1:5–11). We believe in the autonomy of the local churches, free of any external authority and control (Acts 13:1–4, 15:19–31, 20:28; Rom. 16:1, 4; 1 Cor. 3:9, 16; 5: 4–7, 13; 1 Peter 5:1–4). We recognize believer's baptism and the Lord's Supper as scriptural means of testimony for the church (Matt. 28:19, 20; Acts 2:41, 42; 18:8; 1 Cor. 11:23–26).

http://marshill.com/what-we-believe

CHURCH OF GOD IN CHRIST

The church forms a spiritual unity of which Christ is the divine head. It is animated by one spirit, the spirit of Christ. It professes one faith, shares one hope, and serves one king. It is the citadel of the truth and God's agency for communicating to believers all spiritual blessings.

http://www.cogic.org/our-foundation/what-we-believe/

CHURCH OF THE NAZARENE

We believe in the Church, the community that confesses Jesus Christ as Lord, the covenant people of God made new in Christ, the Body of Christ called together by the Holy Spirit through the Word.

God calls the Church to express its life in the unity and fellowship of the Spirit; in worship through the preaching of the Word, observance of the sacraments, and ministry in His name; by obedience to Christ, holy living, and mutual accountability.

The mission of the Church in the world is to [continue] share in the redemptive and reconciling ministry [work] of Christ in the power of the Spirit [through holy living, evangelism, discipleship, and service]. The Church fulfills its mission by making disciples through evangelism, education, showing compassion, working for justice, and bearing witness to the kingdom of God.

The Church is a historical reality, which organizes itself in culturally conditioned forms; exists both as local congregations and as a universal body; sets apart persons called of God for specific ministries. God calls the Church to live under His rule in anticipation of the consummation at the coming of our Lord Jesus Christ.

(Exodus 19:3; Jeremiah 31:33; Matthew 8:11; 10:7; 16:13-19, 24; 18:15-20; 28:19-20; John 17:14-26; 20:21-23; Acts 1:7-8; 2:32-47; 6:1-2; 13:1; 14:23; Romans 2:28-29; 4:16; 10:9-15; 11:13-32; 12:1-8; 15:1-3; 1 Corinthians 3:5-9; 7:17; 11:1, 17-33; 12:3, 12-31; 14:26-40; 2 Corinthians 5:11-6:1; Galatians 5:6, 13-14; 6:1-5, 15; Ephesians 4:1-17; 5:25-27; Philippians 2:1-16; 1 Thessalonians 4:1-12; 1 Timothy 4:13; Hebrews 10:19-25; 1 Peter 1:1-2, 13; 2:4-12, 21; 4:1-2, 10-11; 1 John 4:17; Jude 24; Revelation 5:9-10)

http://nazarene.org/ministries/administration/visitorcenter/articles/display.html

WORLD HARVEST CHURCH

The Church (capital "c") is the fellowship of all Christians around the world. All men and women who have sincerely accepted Jesus Christ as Lord (ruler) and Savior (salvation-maker) of their lives are members of what is also called the body of Christ and the family of God. As in any other family, we can disagree about many things, but also as in any other family, when we have the same father, we have a common bond that never goes away.

The church (small "c") is also the most common term for an individual body of Christian believers…. more than just a building, a church is a community of faithful men and women united to worship God together and make him known to others in a variety of ways.

http://whclife.com/WhatWeBelieve.aspx

MORAVIAN CHURCH

The Moravian church is a Christ-centered church with an active congregational fellowship and service.

The roots of our congregational life are in Christ. Moravian churches are gatherings of believers who take seriously these words of the apostle Paul to the Colossians: "since you have accepted Christ Jesus as Lord, live in union with him. Keep your roots deep in him, build your lives on him and become stronger in your faith." (Colossians 2:6-7 tev).

Our faith identity is as Christians, as followers of Christ who happen to be affiliated with the Moravian church as a way of being Christian. We are Christians first, not Moravians first. Fellowship and service are dual values that flow of our Christ-centeredness, that emerge from the unifying power of God's love alive in our midst.

http://www.moravian.org/the-moravian-church/the-moravian-church/the-moravian-church-is.html

SUMMIT CHURCH (SOUTHERN BAPTIST)

We believe that Jesus established his body on earth in the church and that the church is a community that exists for the purpose of declaring the gospel and glory of Jesus throughout the world.
1 Cor 12:12-31; Col 1:18-20; 1 Peter 2:9

We believe the church is a family and that every believer should be identified with a local body of believers for the purpose of mutual encouragement, spiritual growth and accountability.
Eph 4:11-16; Col 3:12-27; Heb 10:24-25

http://www.summitrdu.com/about/welcome/what-we-believe/

JERRY BROWN, PHD. (Missionary of the Assemblies of God)

The Church is:

- A Colony of the kingdom where Jesus exercises his rule and authority;
- The Temple of the Triune God where He dwells in the midst of his people;
- A prophetic community of the Spirit-born, Spirit-led, Spirit-empowered people of God;
- God's communication medium through which he offers reconciliation to the world through its prophetic proclamation and lifestyle that incarnates the gospel.

CHRISTIAN REFORMED CHURCH

From Our World Belongs to God: A Contemporary Testimony.

35. The Church is the fellowship of those who confess Jesus as Lord. She is the bride of Christ, his chosen partner, loved by Jesus and loving him: delighting in his presence, seeking him in prayer — silent before the mystery of his love.

36. Our new life in Christ is celebrated and nourished in the fellowship of congregations, where we praise God's name, hear the word proclaimed, learn God's ways, confess our sins, offer our prayers and gifts, and celebrate the sacraments.

39. The Church is a gathering of forgiven sinners called to be holy. Saved by the patient grace of God, we deal patiently with others and together confess our need for grace and forgiveness. Restored in Christ's presence, shaped by his life, this new community lives out the ongoing story of God's reconciling love, announces the new creation, and works for a world of justice and peace.

http://www.crcna.org/welcome/beliefs/contemporary-testimony/our-world-

ENDNOTES

1. Brunner, p.108
2. Fulgham, p. 72
3. Barna, p.19
4. Frost and Hirsch, p. 188
5. Andy Stanley, Reggie Joiner, and Lane Jones, p. 33
6. Cyril of Jerusalem, *Procatechesis* (Prologue).
7. Malphurs, p. 132
8. Clinton, p. 14
9. Nouwen, p. 86-87
10. Quinn, p. 179-180
11. Sanders, p. 23
12. Clinton, p.101
13. Callahan, p. 6
14. Hall, p. 161-162
15. Shenk and Stutzman, p. 176-178
16. Hesselgrave, *Planting*, p. 277
17. Greenway, p. 182-200
18. Schwarz, p. 24
19. Larson and LaFasto, summary of book.
20. Healey, J. (unknown source)
21. Malphurs, *Planting*, p. 153
22. Wagner, p. 78
23. Hesselgrave, Planting, p. 107
24. Blackaby, p. 73
25. Brian Kluth, www.kluth.org
26. Tim Keller, Center, p. 89
27. *Ibid*, p. 127
28. *Ibid*, p. 120
29. Hesselgrave, *Communicating*, p. 197ff
30. Keller, Center, p. 123.

31. Hewett, p. 178

32. Rocke and Van Dyke, p. 80-81

33. Choung, website

34. Malphurs, p. 275

35. *Ibid*, p. 207ff

36. Frost and Hirsch, p. 50

37. Shaw and Van Engen, p. 179-180

38. Michael Green, cited in Wagenveld, p. 263

39. José Martinez, cited in Wagenveld, p. 265-269

40. Hudson Taylor, *Historymakers* website

41. Hesselgrave, *Communicating*, 224

42. Henry, Commentary on 1 Timothy 4

43. Snyder, p. 118

44. Kuyper, *see website in bibliography*

45. Scherer and Bevans, p. 278-280

46. Keller, *Generous*, p. 97

47. Burke, http://en.wikiquote.org/wiki/Talk:Edmund_Burke

48. Moore, p. 225

49. Sande, *summary of book*

50. Ham, http://www.worldofquotes.com/quote/40912/index.html

51. Stott, p. 7-8

52. Easum, p. 49

53. *"Nairobi Statement on Worship and Culture."*

54. Stauffer, p. 23-28

55. Hesselgrave, *Communicating*, p. 231

56. Malphurs, *Planting*, 203

57. Pratt, p.179

58. Piper, p. 17

59. Moore, p. 102

60. Hiebert et al, p. 374

61. Wright, p. 98-99

BIBLIOGRAPHY

Barna, George. *The Frog and the Kettle. Delight*, AK: Gospel Light Publications, 1990.

Blackaby, Henry and Claude King. *Experiencing God*. Nashville, Tennessee: Broadman & Holman Publishers, 1994.

Brunner, Emil. *The Word and the World*. University of Virginia: Student Christian Press, 1931.

Burke, Edmund. *Good Reads Inc.* "Edmund Burke Quotes." Accessed December 16, 2013. http://www.goodreads.com/author/quotes/17142.Edmund_Burke.

Callahan, Kennon L. *Effective Church Leadership: Building on the Twelve Keys*. San Francisco: Harper & Row, 1990.

Choung, James. Accessed December 16, 2003. http://www.jameschoung.net/resources/big-story/

Clinton, Robert. *The Making of a Leader*. Colorado Springs.: NavPress, 1988.

Cyril of Jerusalem. "Procatechesis (Prologue)." *New Advent.org*, ed. Kevin Knight. Last modified 2009.

Easum, William M. *The Church Growth Handbook*. Nashville: Abingdon Press, 1990.

Frost, Michael, and Alan Hirsch. *The Shaping of Things to Come: Innovation and Mission for the 21st-Century Church*. Peabody, MA: Hendrickson Publishers, 2003.

Fulgham, Robert. *It Was On Fire When I Lay Down On It*. New York: Random House Publishing Group, 1989.

Green, Michael. *La Iglesia Local: Agente de Evangelización*. Nueva Creación, Grand Rapids, MI: 1996.

Greenway, Roger S. *The Pastor-Evangelist: Preacher, Model, and Mobilizer for Church Growth. Phillipsburg*, N.J.: Presbyterian Reformed Pub. Co., 1987.

Hall, John. *Urban Ministry Factors in Latin America*. Ann Arbor, Michigan: UMI Dissertation Information Service, 1992.

Ham, William. *Daily Christian Quote*. Accessed December 16, 2013. http://dailychristianquote.com/dcqfellowship.html.

Healey, J. Source unknown. Also found in http://thecreativepunk. familylife.ws/blog/2011/12/use-your-ministry-to-build-people-not-people-to-build-your-ministry/

Henry, Matthew. *Exposition of the Old and New Testament Vol. 3*. London:J.R. and C. Childs, 1791.

Hesselgrave, David J. *Planting Churches Cross-Culturally: North America and Beyond*. 2nd ed. Grand Rapids, MI: Baker Books, 2000.

Hesselgrave, David J. *Communication Christ Cross-Culturually: An Introduction to Missionary Communication*. Grand Rapids, MI: Zondervan, 1991.

Hewett, James S. *Illustrations Unlimited*. Wheaton: Tyndale House Publishers, Inc, 1988.

Hiebert, Paul, and Daniel Shaw and Tite Tienou. *Understanding Folk Religion*. Grand Rapids, MI: Baker Books, 1999.

"Hudson Taylor." History Makers: *The Fuel of Missions Flame*. Accessed December 16, 2013. http://www.historymakers.info/ search.&searchword=The+Great+Commission

Keller, Timothy J. *Generous Justice: How God's Grace Makes Us Just*. New York: Dutton, Penguin Group USA, 2010.

Keller, Timothy J. *Center Church: Doing Balanced, Gospel Centered Ministry in Your City*. Grand Rapids, MI: Zondervan, 2012.

Kluth, Brian. *Maximum Generosity*. Accessed on December 16, 2013. www.kluth.org. http://www.kluth.org/church/Quips%20 &%20Quotes.pdf

Kuyper, Abraham. *Good Reads Inc*. "Abraham Kuyper Quotes." Accessed December 16, 2013. www.goodreads.com.

Larson, Carl E., and Frank M. J. LaFasto. *Teamwork: What Must Go Right, What Can Go Wrong*. Newbury Park, CA: SAGE Publications, 1989.

"Nairobi Statement on Worship and Culture." *Calvin Institute of Christian Worship*. Accessed December 16, 2013. http://worship. calvin.edu/resources/resource-library/nairobi-statement-on-worship-and-culture/

Malphurs, Aubrey. *Planting Growing Churches for the 21st Century: A Comprehensive Guide for New Churches and Those Desiring Renewal*. 2nd ed. Grand Rapids, MI: Baker Books, 1998.

Moore, Ralph. *Starting a New Church: The Church Planter's Guide to Success*. Ventura, CA: Regal Books, 2002.

Myers, Bryant L. *Walking with the Poor: Principles and Practices of Transformational Development*. Maryknoll, NY: Orbis Books, 1999.

Nouwen, Henri. *In the Name of Jesus: Reflections on Christian Leadership*. New York: Crossroad Publishing Company, 1989.

Osborne, Larry. "*Creativity and Innovation in Leadership*." A doctoral class at Trinity Evangelical Divinity School, Chicago: 2002.

Piper, John. Let the Nations be Glad!: *The Supremacy of God in Missions*. Grand Rapids, MI: Baker Academic, 2010.

Pratt, Richard L. *Pray With Your Eyes Open: Looking at God, Ourselves, and Our Prayers*. Phillipsburg, NJ: Presbyterian and Reformed Publishing Company, 1987.

Quinn, Robert. Change the World: *How Ordinary People Can Accomplish Extraordinary Results*. San Francisco: Jossey-Bass, 2000.

Rocke, Kris, and Joel Van Dyke. *Geography of Grace: Doing Theology From Below*. United States: Street Psalms Press, 2012.

Sande, Ken. *The Peacemaker: a Biblical Guide to Resolving Personal Conflict*. 2nd ed. Grand Rapids, MI: Baker Books, 1997.

Sanders, Oswald. *Spiritual Leadership: Principles of Excellence for Every Believer*. Chicago: Moody, 1994.

Scherer, James and Stephen Bevans. *New Directions in Mission and Evangelization*. Maryknoll, New York: Orbis Books, 1992.

Schwarz, Christian. *Natural Church Development*. Carol Stream, IL: ChurchSmart Resources, 1996.

Shaw, R. Daniel and Charles Van Engen. *Communicating God's Word in a Complex World*. Lanham, Maryland: Rowman & Littlefield Publishers, Inc., 2003.

Shenk, David W., and Ervin R. Stutzman. *Creating Communities of the Kingdom New Testament Models of Church Planting*. Scottdale, PA: Herald Press, 1988.

Snyder, Howard. *Perspectives on the World Christian Movement*. Edited by Ralph Winter and Steven C. Hawthorne. Pasadena, CA: William Carey Library, 1992.

Stanley, Andy, Reggie Joiner, and Lane Jones. *7 Practices of Effective Ministry*. Sisters, OR: Multnomah Publishers, 2004.

Stauffer, Anita S. *Christian Worship: Unity in Cultural Diversity*. Geneva: Lutheran World Federation, 1996.

Stott, John. *Señales de una Iglesia Viva*. Indef y Certeza, Buenos Aires, 1997.

Van Gelder, Craig. *The Essence of the Church: A Community Created by the Spirit*. Grand Rapids, MI: Baker Book House, 2000.

Wagenveld, John (ed.) *Sembremos Iglesias Saludables*. Miami: FLET, Unilit, 2004.

Wagner, Peter. *Church Planting for a Greater Harvest*. Ventura, CA: Regal Books, 1990.

Wright, N.T. *Evil and the Justice of God*. Downers Grove, IL: InterVarsity Press, 2006.

ABOUT THE AUTHORS

JOHN WAGENVELD is the Executive Director of the Multiplication Network following 20 years of experience in church planting and church planter training.

TIM KOSTER currently serves as pastor of the Emmanuel Christian Reformed Church, (Chicago, USA) his fourth church in 25 years of ordained ministry.

Tim grew up in Michigan, USA and was called to ministry as the son of a small business man with a heart for God and the church, while John grew up in Argentina as a missionary kid. Tim received his Masters in Divinity from Calvin Theological Seminary and John earned a doctorate from Trinity Evangelical Divinity School.

Tim and John and many others have built an informal network of trainers to conduct simple workshops relating to church planting and church health. Based on an open source model, there was a threefold goal of making everything – freely accessible, high quality, and easily reproducible. This movement eventually incorporated into Multiplication Network Ministries (MNM). John devotes fulltime energies to directing MNM while Tim serves as the Board Chair and pastor of the local church where they both worship. Having started in Latin America in 2000, MNM has since expanded to Europe, Africa and Asia.

After church planting in Puerto Rico, John authored the book, *Wholistic Church Growth*, which was published in Spanish. He led the team of 22 authors who joined together to produce the book, *Planting Healthy Churches*, and then edited the compilation. This is Tim's first publication.

John and his wife Angela are actively raising four children. Tim and his wife Mary have four adult children. John loves the game of soccer and plays it whenever he has the opportunity. Tim prefers the "more biblical" avocation of fishing.

Multiplication Network Ministries envisions a healthy church representing the kingdom of God in every community. To do this Christian leaders are trained and equipped to strengthen and multiply healthy churches.

multiplication network

more churches, stronger churches

If you would like to contact the authors please write
www.multiplicationnetwork.org
or call 708-414-1050.
